LIFE OF MAMMA M

Mother of Don

By TERESIO BOSCO SDB

Don Bosco Publications

Italian © 2005 Editrice ELLEDICI – Leumann (Torino)

English © 2006 Don Bosco Publications Bolton England

Translated from the Italian by Julian Fox SDB
Edited by Don Bosco Publications

ISBN 0-9548388-5-8
Don Bosco Publications

Thornleigh House
Sharples Park
BOLTON BL1 6PQ
England
Tel: 01204 308811
Fax: 01204 306868
www.don-bosco-publications.co.uk

CONTENTS

PRESENTATION

Jesus was nailed to a Cross on Golgotha, stripped of everything. The only item he still had on this earth, his tunic, ended up in the hands of the soldiers. However at that supreme moment, Jesus acknowledged someone who was especially dear to him, his mother. He said to the disciple who was with her, and to all humanity, *Behold, your mother.* At this point he had given away everything.

We see how Don Bosco had made those words of Jesus his own. He often used to say to his boys, *Everything, absolutely everything, right up to my last breath, I give for you.* For this reason, like Jesus, along with his own life he gave his mother to his boys, to the Congregation and to all the Salesian Family.

Just as Mary is an inestimable gift for the Church, Mamma Margaret is a gift that we have not yet finished discovering for the Salesian Family. We have no doubts today about the important role Mamma Margaret had in the human and Christian upbringing of Don Bosco, as she also had in the creation of the educative atmosphere of Valdocco. Her maternal presence certainly contributed to making the atmosphere in Valdocco a family one. Thanks to her, Don Bosco's robust fatherliness was in harmony with the understanding, kindness, attention and affection hidden in a mother's heart. This is the fascination of the Salesian educational system.

Fr Egidio Viganò expressed it in these words:
> Mamma Margaret's heroic transfer to Valdocco saw the atmosphere for those boys steeped in the same family style from which the substance of the Preventive System has sprung. So many of our traditions are associated with it. Don Bosco's experience was that the formation of his personality was vitally rooted in the extraordinary climate of self-giving and goodness in his family, in The Becchi, and he wanted to reproduce its most significant qualities in the Valdocco Oratory amongst those poor and abandoned boys.

Don Bosco's first memory is holding his mother's hand when she accompanied little John from the room where his father had breathed his last. He himself tells the story:
> *Poor child*, my mother said, *come with me, you no longer have a papa.* That said, she broke into tears, took me by the hand and led me elsewhere, while I was crying because she was crying.

Margaret tormented by sorrow and apprehension about the future, is kind and firm: she will never leave her children.

We are preparing to celebrate the 150 years since her death, in Turin, November 25th 1856. Her attractive personality can become a stimulus for strengthening our option for an education based on kindness, the key to the heart. It is also a model for mothers and families today.

Margaret Occhiena is a thoroughly modern mother: She carried the weight of the family on her shoulders. A classic line about mothers today might go like this: The mother is always on her own! Today, mothers are on their own in many ways. They have a double task: at home and at work, or because they are separated or left with the children, or because, as in many cases, they are left alone in the task of bringing up the children.

Mamma Margaret was especially present among the boys of the Oratory who felt they were her children, as much as Don Bosco was. Hers was a total and effective love, made up of words and many deeds. A constant example of complete self-giving. She was illiterate, but rich in an infinite wisdom and common sense.

I am grateful to Fr Teresio Bosco for this reason, because he has painted so vividly in these pages a Mamma Margaret who is alive and close to us. They allow our Salesian Family to rediscover one of its most important roots. In Mamma Margaret's life, pedagogical teachings and catechism are never theories, but arise directly from her experience of life, from her simple words, wise and full of faith and Christian wisdom. In their substance, those teachings remain valid, not dated. They say something wonderful and constructive to mothers today.

We hope that 2006 gives us the grace of seeing her heroic virtues recognised, and perhaps even her Beatification, because, based on the words of Pope Benedict XVI, *Mamma Margaret's holiness is so evident, that it would not even require the full process.*

Rome, November 25th 2005
Fr Pascual Chávez Villanueva
Rector Major of the Salesians

5

1. A Little Girl in Bandit Land

Margaret was born on April 1st 1788 to the Occhiena family from Capriglio. Her first loud squeals spoke volumes about her will to live. Her mother Domenica smiled as she listened to that first loud cry. This was her sixth child and Domenica and her husband Melchior were glad, almost all her little sisters and brothers, Mary, Julia, Teresa and John had died within a short time of birth. In those days infant mortality, as much for farmers as for royalty, carried off twenty-five percent of children in their first year of life, and a further twenty-five percent over the following four years.

At baptism, which she received the same day, she was called Margaret, a popular name at the time. It means *precious stone,* and for country folk it meant that little daisy-like flower with white petals, dewy and soft, a tiny yellow sun shining at its centre. While the priest poured water on her head, making Margaret a Christian, little wide-eyed, three-year-old Marianna, her only surviving sister, stared at her. They would be the best of friends for the rest of their lives.

A Troop of Russian Soldiers

Margaret would discover, much later, that one year after she was born the French Revolution began, an event that would change the world with its triple call for *Liberty, Equality, Fraternity*, under the bloodstained shadow of the guillotine. That Revolution would also engulf her own peaceful little village. When she was nine she learned that the young French general, Napoleon Bonaparte, had invaded her territory of Piedmont, bringing war and destruction to the province of Asti, to which Capriglio belonged. War and guerrilla activity would last another ten years.

As a young eleven-year-old she was sent to look after the ears of corn laid out to dry in the sun. One day she saw a troop of Russian soldiers on horseback arrive in the yard. In the fight against Napoleon they laid waste homes and the countryside. The horses went for the ears of corn that Margaret was looking after, and began munching them with their huge teeth. At first Margaret shouted and waved her arms to frighten them off, then she turned on their riders with her fierce, young tongue. They stood there in a group and laughed at her rage. Infuriated by their attitude, she grabbed a pitchfork and began attacking their horses. The horses ran away, their riders in hot pursuit for fear of losing them.

Where Bandits Ruled

In those years of war and guerrilla activity, Piedmont became *bandit territory.* The ten-year-old Margaret often heard her father and her uncles speaking in trepidation about these lawless men. They claimed to be on the side of the King or the French, or indeed the Pope himself, but they massacred and set fire to whole villages. Margaret knew these bandits had attacked Asti, killed French soldiers and ransacked the churches, the taverns and the seminary. All this she had heard the men of the village recount in whispers. A curious child doesn't miss much.

In May 1799 the French soldiers were chasing the bandits as they ran wild throughout the countryside, shooting anyone, burning down farmsteads, and killing women and children. The bandits were a loose pack under the command of a certain Branda de Lucioni. They had adopted the name, *The Gang of Christians*, but were distinctly unchristian with their random attacks and vicious vendettas. Armed with an assortment of guns or even just forks, rakes or hoes, they attacked the French soldiers wherever they found them. The latter responded by setting fire to the countryside. The people had to flee to the woods. Then *The Gang of Christians* moved towards Turin to *liberate* it, but everywhere they provoked terror. Nobody wanted these bloodthirsty bandits as allies. Some years later Branda was arrested and thrown into prison. Some of his mob continued causing havoc along the borders between Piedmont and Liguria.

Piedmont Becomes Part of France

In 1801 Napoleon declared Piedmont to be the 27th *Military Division of France,* divided into six *départements.* He imposed the French language and law, and Piedmontese troops were incorporated into the French army. Margaret saw the first young men from Capriglio drafted into the French army.

She saw many more men depart in 1812, to the great consternation of their families. They were pressed into service by Napoleon for his expedition against Russia. He invaded that distant and mysterious country with the greatest army of all time. During the rigorous Moscow winter, however, he suffered a serious defeat, and began a disastrous retreat. Of the 600,000 men of Napoleon's army who perished in that ill-fated campaign, 25,000 were Italians.

2. Youthful Years

Capriglio was a little village, of 400 inhabitants, located on a tiny plateau, surrounded by the undulating green hills of Monferrato. The houses at that time were grouped around the castle belonging to Count Radicati Passerano. Today Capriglio has no castle.

Margaret Occhiena was born in the hamlet known as *Cecca*, buried amongst the green woods, its sunny hills cultivated with vines. From the windows of her home, Margaret could see the valley through which ran a small brook, which eventually emptied into the Traversa stream. Beyond, she could see the roofs of houses in Morialdo, with The Becchi district and the extensive farming land of the Biglione family of lawyers. She couldn't have imagined that one day, in her wedding dress, she would cross that valley, and become the mother of two children in that district.

Margaret's First Words

Margaret lived a happy childhood in that solid and rustic little farmhouse despite the tragic days when the soldiers and bandits visited those hills. Under the kindly eye of her mother and grandmother, she played and laughed with Marianna and the other little brothers and sisters the Lord had sent them, Francis, Lucia and Michael. Like all young children they were happy to be with the chickens and the geese, pulling the cats' tails, and chasing the doves till they took flight.

Margaret never went to school. Country girls, at that time, were not even taught to read and write. Nor did she go to nursery, since nurseries had not been invented, and there wasn't any need since every farmyard, filled with the children from two or three families, was already a crowded nursery, and they socialised daily without even knowing the meaning of the word. The priests came along to bless the homes and to offer words of encouragement. The first words their mothers taught the children were those of the Hail Mary.

The Village Street

The village of Capriglio had a main road running right through it, from one end to the other, bordered by chestnuts, acacias and mulberry trees. The young girls of the village used to spend long hours on the road, laughing, chatting, arm-in-arm as they walked. They were there to be looked at, to attract the attention of the young men gathered under the trees. They moved around in large numbers, from house to house, inviting their friends to join them. As they passed Margaret's house they would call on her loudly to join them. *Come on Margaret, come along. We're going to have some fun.*

Margaret could see, from the look on her mother's face, that she wasn't keen on her joining in their fun. Her mother wanted to keep Margaret under her watchful eye, and Margaret knew it. So she would look for excuses, *I've already been for a walk today, and I'm rather tired. I went to Mass with my mother, and you know how far it is, there and back, to the church.*

The Village Dance

In summer, every village celebrated its special feast day. There was a solemn Mass during the day and a procession. In the evening, music could be heard as people gathered for the dance in the open air. As music echoed from hillside to hillside, it was an irresistible invitation for the young people. At that time, all the priests were opposed to the dance as a way of celebrating the feast. The local parish priest was loud in his condemnation of the dance. Margaret was, of course, regularly invited. She would courteously decline the invitation.

The Ideal

By the time she was eighteen years old, Margaret was a very attractive young woman. She had her admirers. Many a young man sought the company of Margaret. They were even prepared to walk with her as she made the long journey every Sunday to the parish church for Mass. She would smile graciously at their advances, but, in fact, they annoyed her. She tried so many ways to deter them. She tried walking fast to tire them out, or leaving home early, well before the time for Mass.

Finally she discovered a solution. There was a very bad-tempered old lady who was always looking for someone to help her on her way to Mass. She used to struggle along with her walking stick. Margaret began to go with her each Sunday to and from Mass. When young men joined them, the old lady would shout at them, and wave her stick at them. Reluctantly, they finally had to give up.

3. Wife and Mother

About the age of twenty, Margaret's best friends were already married or getting ready for marriage. Margaret instead, was taking her time. She felt obliged to stay with her father and mother, to help them in their old age. Her father Melchior tried to persuade her otherwise, *Your mother and I are in good health, thanks be to God. You have all the qualities to become a good wife and mother.*

In 1811, in the nearby hamlet of The Becchi, Francis Bosco, a tenant farmer, had lost his wife. His infant child, Teresa, had died the previous year. Francis was already a widower at 27 years of age. He still had one small child, Anthony, just three years old. Little Anthony had been so traumatised by the sight of his dead mother; he was entrusted to his grandmother, who was an invalid.

The Occhiena family had known Francis Bosco for some time, because he often came to Capriglio to help his cousin, Maddalena. She was a widow. Francis had often stopped to chat with Melchior, to talk about sowing and harvesting. Francis had also met and exchanged a few words with Melchior's daughter, Margaret.

Once the mourning period was over, Francis decided to come to Capriglio to ask Melchior for his daughter's hand in marriage. Melchior surprised Francis by being very open to the idea; the family had already discussed the possibility. During the days that followed, he spoke with his wife Domenica. Then they called in Margaret and told her of Francis' request, *If you are in agreement, we are too. Clearly you will be part of a family that is poorer than ours, but Francis is a wonderful Christian and a hard worker. It will not be a great wedding because the family is going through a time of suffering. You will have to care for a young child; you will be both wife and mother.* Margaret accepted.

The marriage was celebrated in Capriglio on June 6th 1812. In accordance with Napoleonic law they went to the registry office first, where the marriage was registered in French. Immediately afterwards, the religious ceremony was celebrated in their church. On the wedding day itself Margaret, 24 years of age, put on her beautiful wedding gown and the simple jewels given her by her mother and father. Then, she immediately packed them all away in her little trunk, and set off to live with her new family in The Becchi district, in the country cottage of Francis, next to the Biglione farmstead.

Anthony

Margaret began a new life, poor but happy. Grandma, also called Margaret, kissed her on both cheeks, welcoming her as one of the Lord's blessings. Anthony, barely four years old, allowed himself to be picked up and hugged by his new *Mamma*, even though the poor boy must have been very confused.

Francis did not want to spend all his life as a tenant farmer. His dream, like that of so many farmers in those days, was to become a farmer in his own right, with his own home and his own land. By living frugally he was able to buy a piece of land and a small vineyard, a mere 1900 square metres. Then he bought some animals, which he kept, initially, in the stable of his father-in-law, Melchior. After some time he bought a small shed on credit, and fixed it up for his work tools, also a stable and a hayloft for the two oxen and the cow he had been keeping at Melchior's place. He was not worried about the debt. Instead he worked away at lowering it, bit by bit, through hard work.

Margaret and Francis, however, did not bury their life completely in work. Michael Rua, as a boy in Turin, spent four years with Mamma Margaret and became one of the first Salesians, later he testified:

> Don Bosco's parents were excellent Christians, endowed with good sense through the religious instruction they picked up as part of parish religious teaching. This I heard from Don Bosco's mother and from Don Bosco himself. With regard to his mother, since I lived with her for four years, I came to know her as a truly pious Christian woman, generous of heart, courageous and prudent.

Four Happy Years

On April 8th 1813 Margaret and Francis' first child was born. When he was baptised, he was named Joseph. On August 16th 1815 the second child, John, was born. Don Bosco, in his memoirs, wrote of his mother and father:

> They were farmers who earned their living by hard work and thrifty use of what little they had. My good father, almost entirely by the sweat of his brow, was responsible for three youngsters of whom the oldest was Anthony, born of his first wife, the second was Joseph, and the youngest was me, John. He also supported my grandmother in her seventies. She was a prey to frequent illnesses.

For four years life smiled kindly on this little family. Margaret was a radiantly happy woman with her young sons. Francis was a cheerful, energetic farmer. He would return home from the fields towards evening exhausted, but glad to hold his children in his arms.

Madonna dei Bastioni

Health in those days and in those hilly regions, was a precarious thing. Later, Mamma Margaret would say to John, *When you came into the world, I consecrated you to the Blessed Virgin.* At a time when death carried off fifty percent of newly born infants this was a religious act. At two to three years of age children, then as now, were prone to the usual illnesses: chickenpox, measles and mumps. These are easily cured or prevented today, but then, they were often fatal. When a child seemed seriously ill, their mothers would often take them to the Shrine of the Madonna dei Bastioni, in Villanova d'Asti. Mamma Margaret too, it seems, had brought her young son John to the shrine, suffering from a high fever: His name can be seen there, engraved at the foot of a pillar.

Adults were not immune to life-threatening illnesses. A new disease had recently arrived, one that terrified people: the plague. It afflicted those who lived almost exclusively on *polenta* made from corn, the bread of the poor. The spring of 1817 brought typhoid fever, a disease that came from drinking contaminated water. It was a very contagious disease, devastating the villages around Turin. Francis Bosco died in the prime of his life in 1817, from pneumonia.

4. The Death of Margaret's Husband

In his memoirs Don Bosco records the death of his father:
I was not yet two years old, when our family suffered a sad bereavement. My father was strong and healthy, still young and actively engaged in giving us a good Christian upbringing. One day, returning from work drenched in sweat, without thinking, he went down into the cold cellar. He was struck down by a high fever, the first signs of serious pneumonia. All attempts to cure him were to no avail. Within a few days the illness had brought him to the point of death. In his final hours he received the Sacraments and entrusted my mother to God. He was 34 years old when he died. It was May 11th 1817.
I only have one memory of those days, the first memory of my life: everyone had left the room where my father had died, but I didn't want to follow them. My mother said to me, *Come on John, come with me.*
I replied, *If papa is not coming, I'm not coming.*
My mother said, *Poor child, you no longer have a papa.* Saying that, she burst into tears, took me by the hand and led me out. I was crying too, but only because I saw her crying. At that age, I could not understand what a tragedy had befallen us in our father's death. This event threw the whole family into chaos.[1]
Recalling this event in later years when talking to his boys, he would add, *I will always remember those words, You no longer have a papa.* On one occasion, Dominic Ruffino was there and wrote it down. Don Bosco said, *I also recall what my brother and I did at home on that occasion. He was overcome with sorrow.* Poor Anthony, now nine years old, had seen first his mother die, now his father.

Mamma Margaret in Court

When her husband died, John Bosco's mother Margaret was only 29 years old. She was young enough to cope with three sons and her semi-paralysed mother-in-law. She was left with a vineyard and land just sufficient for survival, with a shack which needed to be converted from a stable to a dwelling. She did not spend many days feeling sorry for herself. She rolled up her sleeves and went back to work.

From May to November, Margaret, with help from two farmhands, successfully completed the tenant-farmer's season of duty. She managed to save the best part of the harvest. After November 11th 1817, the tenant-farmer relationship between the Biglione owners and the Bosco family came to an end. The Biglione family however, in a squalid finale, took the Bosco family to court because they felt the fields had not

---

[1] Memoirs of the Oratory pp 7-8

been cared for and the harvest was less than what had been expected. This family of lawyers prosecuted the young widow who had just buried her husband, who knew neither how to read nor write. Margaret made many journeys to court on foot. The sentence passed on Margaret was a fine of 22.5 lire. This she had to accept by signing in the only way she knew, by making her mark.

During those months, Margaret's brother Michael put everything aside to transform the shed from a stable into a basic cottage, and Mamma Margaret, her three sons and their grandmother moved in. Despite Michael's efforts, the cottage was the poorest house in that area.

This was a most difficult time for Margaret. She had lost her husband; she had abandoned their house to accommodate her three sons and a sick old lady in a shed built to be a stable. She had been summonsed and sentenced by the court. She had to quickly set to work on the plot of land left her by her husband, to keep her children. In March 1818, ten months after losing her husband, she also lost her dear mother Domenica. Whoever understands family life knows how comforting it is for a young wife and mother to have her own mother around. There was enough there for a young twenty-nine-year-old woman to despair. Margaret however had great faith in God and great love for her sons. She did not spend her time lamenting her situation. She once again rolled up her sleeves and set to work.

Margaret's hands were soon blistered by the hard work of ploughing and harvesting, but those same hands knew how to gently caress her children. She was a strong woman, a worker, but remained a mother to her children.

5. Famine

The same year that brought the death of the father of the family, brought misery and famine. After a season, where it had rained incessantly, came a summer without sun. The harvest was poor. The Monferrato hills, like all of Piedmont, Lombardy and Liguria, suffered severe famine. Famine is a vague word, but can be understood when we read the farming statistics of that time. We are told that in a normal season each grain of wheat sown can produce a four- or six-fold return. But during a famine, a grain of wheat would produce two-fold at most. In areas of real famine, beggars would be found dead in a ditch, their mouths stuffed with grass.

Turin, the capital of Piedmont, was described in 1817 as a city invaded by hordes of people who had abandoned the land and come to camp outside churches and the palaces of the rich. The governor of Genoa wrote to the King of Piedmont, *Hunger is destroying entire families*. In Lombardy, the lack of foliage on the mulberry trees meant the end of the cultivation of silkworms, the meagre support for so many farming families.

In The Becchi cottage too, there was fear and hunger. In his memoirs, Don Bosco wrote:

> The crops failed that year because of a drought. The prices of foodstuffs soared. My mother used to tell me that she fed the family until she exhausted all her food. She then had to go to the neighbours to try to borrow something, but nobody was able to help us. Then without losing courage she said, *Papa, when he was dying, told me to trust in God. So let us kneel down and pray.* After a short prayer she got up, then she said, *Drastic circumstances demand drastic measures.* With the help of Bernardo Cavallo, a neighbour, she went to the stable, killed a calf, immediately cooked some of it and gave us supper.[2]

Until not so many decades ago, for Piedmontese families, killing a calf was always a drastic action to take. The calf fattened in the stable was an investment to be sold at the market to overcome very difficult situations such as a family illness or a sudden fire. Don Bosco adds, *In the days that followed, my mother managed to get some cereals from far-off villages but at a very high price.*

This was Mamma Margaret's version of events. The truth was that cereal didn't come from far-off villages, but was bought by a local priest, Don Vittorio Amedei. He sold it to the widow at an exorbitant price, four *emina*[3] at 9.17 lire each, while the official price on the Turin market was 7.43 lire each. Don Bosco wrote:

---

[2] Memoirs of the Oratory p 8

[3] A Piedmontese dry measure of the day. One emina=a quarter of a litre

Anyone can imagine how much my mother worked and suffered in that disastrous year, but the crisis of that year was overcome by constant hard work, by continuous thrift, by attention to the smallest details and by occasional providential help. My mother often told me about these things and my relatives and friends confirmed them.

Another year passed before Margaret was able to settle accounts with the herbalist, Giannella, from Castelnuovo *for the herbs sent for your husband's burial*. She paid him 6.15 lire, a farmer's earnings amounted to one lira a day. In the years to follow, she was only able to pay Montalenti, the notary, by instalments. He had come to The Becchi *to arrange for the details of the will and the goods belonging to Francis Bosco, 32 lire.*

A Mother to Her Sons

When that terrible scarcity was over, and matters at home had improved, a convenient arrangement was proposed to Mamma Margaret. It was suggested to her that her children could be entrusted to a good guardian who would look after them. However, she repeated again and again, *God gave me a husband and God has taken him away; with his death, the Lord put three children under my care. I would be a cruel mother to abandon them just when they needed me most. A guardian could only be their friend, but I am a mother to these sons of mine; all the gold in the world could never make me abandon them.*

Her greatest concern was to instruct her children in their faith, making them value obedience and keeping them busy with tasks suitable to their age.

6. Kind but Firm Love

The first lesson John, Joseph and Anthony learned was their mother's kindly, yet firm, love. A hundred years later, psychologists would write that children, in order to grow up properly, need a father's demanding love and the freely-given love of a mother. Demanding paternal love is what moves us to duty, to accomplishing goals, something that continually exhorts us to be *worthy of our father*. Freely-given maternal love is what gives us a taste for living, not just achieving results; something that gives us consolation in moments of defeat. It reminds us that there is someone who loves us not for what we do but for who we are; for the very fact of being a son or daughter. Mamma Margaret instinctively achieved a balance. She combined a calm firmness with a soothing joy. While being a very kind mother, she was energetic and strong. Her children knew that when she said *No*, she meant *No*. Don Bosco recalls three episodes which throw some light on his mother's kind yet firm love.

The Cane in the Corner

His mother kept a cane in one corner of her kitchen, but never used it. One day John got into serious trouble. Perhaps, in a hurry to go out and play, he left the rabbit hutch open and all the rabbits escaped into the yard. It would be hard work to get them all back in again. Coming back to the kitchen exhausted, Margaret pointed to the corner, *John, go and get me that cane.* The child shrank back towards the door, *What are you going to do with it?* Her tone was decisive. *Bring it here and you'll find out.* John went and retrieved it and leaned across to give it to her, *Are you going to...*

And why not, if you are going to be up to mischief?

Mamma, I won't do it again. At this point, Don Bosco recalls, how his mother laughed. *Stop pulling such a face, don't look so anxious.* She laughed and her son laughed with her. Life in the cottage returned to its quiet, relaxed state.

A Lesson Learned

One very hot day, John and Joseph came back from the vineyard with a raging thirst. Margaret went to the well, pulled up a bucket of cold water, and gave Joseph something to drink first. John, just four, showed his annoyance at the preference given to Joseph. When his mother offered him something to drink, he refused it. Margaret said, *Poor thing, I've left you to last and now you're not happy! Go on, be a good boy.* He said nothing. She carried the bucket into the kitchen and closed the door. A moment later John came in, *Mamma*, he said.

What's the matter? his mother replied.
Aren't you going to give me something to drink?
I thought you weren't thirsty.
I'm really sorry, Mamma.
She gave him the water to drink.

The Carved Stick

Every Thursday, Margaret went to the market in Castelnuovo. She took along two bundles with cheeses, chickens and vegetables to sell. She would come back with cloth, candles, salt and some small presents for the children. As the sun was setting they would go running along the path to meet her.

One Thursday, while his mother was at the market, John, eight years old, ran back to the kitchen, took a chair and on tiptoe, reached up above the cupboard. Maybe he was looking for something to play with. While he was reaching up, disaster struck! The jar of oil on top of the cupboard fell down onto the floor, smashed, and the oil poured out over the red bricks. Joseph, seeing his brother hadn't come back, came to look for him. He saw the oil on the floor. His hand went to his mouth, *Just wait till Mamma comes back.* They tried to clear things up. They got a broom. They tried to pick up the smashed bits and pieces of the jar. The oil had stained the floor, and spread like their fear.

John went very quiet for half an hour. Then he got out a knife, went to the hedge, cut a branch off and set to work on it. At the same time he started thinking. He was trying to work out what he would say to his mother. By the time he had finished, the stick was ready. He had rehearsed in his head all the words he was going to say. At sunset they headed out to meet their mother. Joseph, a bit unsure, lagged behind. John, instead, ran on ahead.
Good evening, Mamma. How are you?
I'm fine. How are you?
He offered her the finely carved stick. *Um, Mamma, look.*
Puzzled she asked, *What have you been up to?*
Ruefully he mumbled, *I've broken the jar of oil.*
He breathlessly told her all about it, and finished off, *I brought you the stick because I really deserve to be punished.*

Margaret looked at him, and could only laugh. *I'm upset about the jar of oil, but I'm glad you didn't come to tell me lies. Next time be careful, think before you act. Oil is very expensive.*

This love, both demanding and calm, is the first educational lesson that would stay with Don Bosco all his life. He had just one source of love, at the same time both paternal and maternal. Don Bosco, in his turn, became the same source of love for his boys. His love, like his mother's, showed a calm firmness and a soothing joy.

The psychologist Giacomo Dacquino has given us an insight into the relationship between John and Mamma Margaret in those early years:

> The profound relationship between mother and child played a determining role in Don Bosco's life. Throughout his life, his mother's words and example would accompany him, as would the trust build in his relationship with her. He made us aware of it when he told us how he related to his companions when he was a young boy. Self-esteem, self-assuredness, awareness of his own qualities are all elements constitutive of the person, and therefore of his power to attract. Little John needed all this to succeed in conducting himself in the presence of adults and those of his own age who listened to him.[4]

---

[4] Psicologia di Don Bosco, pp. 21ss

7. Margaret's Work Ethic

A second lesson John Bosco learned from his mother, a lesson which would last for the rest of his life, was her work ethic. His mother worked, and her children helped as best they could. The Bosco home was poor. Of all The Becchi homes, the Bosco's was the poorest: a ground floor, which served as living quarters, hayloft and stable. In the kitchen the stacks of grain were stored, and beyond a thin wall, were kept two cows.

True poverty then, but not abject poverty, because there was work for all. Farmer's work, though there was little return, was not fruitless labour. The walls were bare, but they were whitewashed. There were only a few sacks of corn, they were emptied slowly, and they were barely sufficient. The Bosco children, therefore, were not harmed by sadness, or by violence, the sad effects of extreme poverty on some children. It is even possible to be poor yet happy, provided we are loved.

John was four years old when his mother gave him the first three or four cuts of hemp to unravel. It wasn't much of a job, but it was work. In this way he began to make his own little contribution to the family, whose survival depended on everyone's work. John was five and Joseph was seven when Margaret sent them to look after and feed the turkeys. While the birds chased crickets, the young brothers played, ran and jumped. But they kept an eye on the turkeys, because their mother had said, *Here's a job for you. Make sure you do it well.*

The Sack in the Hedge

One day, interrupting their game and counting on his fingers, Joseph yelled out that one turkey was missing. They searched frantically. They found nothing. One missing turkey was a serious matter, it just couldn't disappear that easily. Running to the other side of the hedge, John saw a man. It suddenly occurred to him, *He's stolen it.* He called Joseph over and determinedly they approached the man, *Give us back that turkey.* The stranger looked at them in surprise, *A turkey? What turkey?* The boys said, *You've stolen it. Come on, give it back. Otherwise we'll cry 'thief' and people will take a stick to you.* Could two children really deal with him? Their determination made him ill at ease. There were farmers at work nearby. *If these boys start shouting, I'm in real trouble,* he thought. He pulled the sack out of the hedge, and took out the turkey. *I was only playing a joke on you*, he said. The boys shouted, *It's not a very Christian kind of joke.* He ran away. That evening, as always, they gave an account of the day to their mother. *You took a risk*, she said. *Why*? They answered. *You weren't sure it was him.* She said. *But there wasn't anybody else close by. This is not enough to go calling someone a thief. You are just small boys, he is a grown man. What if he'd hurt you?* John would not be silenced, *Should we have let him take the turkey?* His mother remarked wisely. *It's good to be brave, but it's better to lose a turkey than to come back home hurt.* John mumbled thoughtfully, *Um… As you wish, Mamma. But it was a big fat turkey.*

The Value of Work

Between eight and nine years of age, John began to take a more active part in family work. He began to share the austere and difficult life style. They would work from dawn to dusk, and the sun rises early in summer. Margaret would say to her children as she was waking them in the morning, *A sleeping man never catches fish.* Breakfast was simple fare: a slice of dry bread and cold water. John learned to hoe, mow the grass, use the clippers and milk the cows like any true farmer. Since all journeys were on foot, the long road to Castelnuovo was itself hard work.

In the evening, as he fell asleep on the mattress stuffed with corn leaves, John felt the deep satisfaction of playing an active part in his family, overcoming its difficulties, because he, too, was lending a hand. He experienced a sense of belonging, of value and dignity. These are things that give life its meaning, and which Don Bosco would hand on to his boys and to his Salesians. In Valdocco, one of the worst things that could be said about a boy was that he was *lazy.* It was synonymous with being *outside the family, a boy without dignity.*

In those years in Chieri and Castelnuovo, John Bosco developed this commitment to work instilled in him by his mother. The six workshops he would build in Valdocco would be the practical translation of this way of seeing things, and his way of encouraging his boys to take pride in their work.

In order to save souls, the ultimate purpose of his life, Don Bosco always saw the absolute necessity for work: the only way of bringing about a saving love. To Bishop Cagliero, in his last years, he would say, *Tell all the Salesians to work with burning zeal: work, work. I am in my final years of life. It is up to you now to work and save young people.*

8. Margaret's God

The third thing John Bosco took from his mother was a sense of God. *God sees you* was Mamma Margaret's most frequent saying. She would leave her children to roam the nearby fields, and as they left she would say, *Remember, God sees you.* If she saw them about to argue, or prepared to tell lies to escape trouble, *Remember, God knows what you are thinking.*

But it wasn't an authoritarian God she introduced to her children. If the night was bright and cloudless, star-filled, she would say to them as they stood outside, *God created the world and put all the stars up there.* When the fields were covered in flowers, she would say, *How many wonderful things the Lord has made for us.* After the crop had ripened, after the harvest, catching her breath again after work, she would say, *Let's give thanks to the Lord. He has been good to us. He has given us our daily bread.* Even when rain and hail had ruined the crops, she invited them to reflect, *The Lord has given, the Lord has taken away.*

John learned to recognise this great person, unseen, but everywhere present: in heaven, in the countryside, in the face of the poor, in his conscience, saying, *You have done well. You have done wrong.* A person in whom his mother had unlimited confidence. A good Father and Provider, someone who gives us our daily bread, sometimes lets things happen to us: the death of a dear one, hailstorms in the vineyard, things at times difficult to understand, but, *He knows why, and that's good enough for us.*

We can see that John Bosco from his earliest years had an image of God filtered through nature: the God of the heavens, the stars, the sun, snow, the trees and the birds. These were aspects of his mother's God, aspects which informed the way she talked about the grass, the hay, the sky, or when, at the Moglia farm, they would go looking for the lost calf. John Bosco never needed a kneeler to pray on. He would just lift up his eyes, look around, and speak to God.

The Family Prays Together

As the years passed, John grew from infant to small boy, to teenager. Margaret also helped him to grow in his understanding of God. She was illiterate, but the parish priest of Capriglio had taught her lengthy verses from the Gospel, and she would repeat them to her children. She believed in the need to pray, to speak with God, in order to gain strength to live and to do good. From family and parish, Margaret had learned a basic collection of prayers and she taught them to her children. *Since I was very young*, Don Bosco wrote, *It was she who taught me to pray. She taught me to kneel down with my brothers, both morning and evening, and together we would say our prayers.*

The parish priest was far away, in Castelnuovo. The nearest church was in Morialdo, but it was only open occasionally when there was a chaplain available. Margaret didn't wait for a priest to find the time to come and teach her boys the catechism.[5] She taught it herself. The Catechism was by Bishop Michael Casati, adapted and added to by Bishop Costa, the bishop of Casale. It was in the style of question and answer, with appropriate and easily learned items. No wonder Mamma Margaret knew the most important pages of the Catechism she had learned in Capriglio by heart, and ensured it was learned by heart at home.[6] Margaret re-learned the catechism in the parish at Castelnuovo, bringing Anthony along for the preparation for his First Communion. With her tenacious farmer's memory, she would recite it and have Joseph and then John recite it.

Mamma Margaret's Catechism

The *Short Catechism for Children* has been preserved in the Turin seminary library. It is an emotional experience to re-read the words passed from Mamma Margaret's lips to her children's alert little minds. Scholar Peter Braido writes:

> For whoever wants to understand the sources of Don Bosco's religious mentality and spirituality, and also his education, it would be hard to exaggerate the influence of the Breve Catechismo which he learned by heart from his mother and from his first religious priest teachers.

Here are some of the questions and answers from *Lesson 1. Concerning the One God*:

> Q. Who created you?
> A. God created me.
> Q. Why did God create you?
> A. To know, love and serve Him in this life, and then to enjoy Him forever in heaven.
> Q. How can we know God in this life?
> A. Through the light of faith and reason.
> Q. How must we know and serve Him in this life?
> A. Through keeping his Commandments, and directing all our actions to His honour and glory.

---

[5] Printed in Turin in 1819 and used by nearby dioceses, including Asti

[6] Positio I, 127

First Confession

At that time, children made their First Communion around 12-14 years of age. Their First Confession was much earlier. Don Bosco records this important event in his Christian life:

> I remember that my mother herself prepared me for my First Confession. She went to church with me, went to confession herself, then presented me to the confessor, and helped me to make my thanksgiving. She continued to do this until I reached the age when she judged me able to use the sacrament well of my own accord.

The Rosary

One of the first religious practices, which John learned, was saying the rosary. In those days it was the evening prayer for all Christians. By repeating the Hail Mary fifty times, farmers of The Becchi also conversed with Our Lady, more a mother than a Queen. For them, it was no problem saying the same words fifty times. During the day they had already hoed the furrows hundreds of times, and they knew you only reaped a good harvest by doing so. By calling on the Madonna's help fifty times over, saying *now and at the hour of our death*, they could reap a spiritual harvest. While they quietly said the Hail Mary, and the little ones fell asleep, they thought of their families, their fields, of the present and the future. John Bosco thus began to converse with Our Lady. He knew that she heard him and looked after him.

John grew up this way, in a family, a small Christian community nurtured by prayer and God's Word. He would soon begin to do the same with his friends. Before finishing his games, he would repeat some thought from the parish priest during the homily. He would take part in the Parish Mission, absorb what he had heard, and repeat it word for word.

9. A Mother's Wisdom

Margaret didn't only teach John to see God in nature. She taught him also to see him in the face of others. If someone was seriously ill in one of the nearby homes, Margaret went to keep an eye on them. She knew one should not refuse to give a helping hand. She would take one of her children along as company. She used to say, *There is a work of charity to be done.* Charity in the Bosco family wasn't a matter of philanthropy or sentiment, but love of God. God dwelt in that house. He came in the guise of those living on the margins.

Beggar's Wooden Shoes

In winter, Don Bosco recalled, *a beggar would often knock on our door. Snow would be all around, and he would ask if he could sleep in the hayloft.* Margaret, before letting him climb up there, would give him a bowl of hot soup. Then she would look at his feet. Most times they would be in bad shape. The worn-out wooden clogs would let in the water and everything else. She didn't have another pair to give him, but she would wrap up his feet in cloth, and bandage them as best she could.

Fugitives in the Woods

There was a wood near the house. More than once, as night fell, small groups of fugitives from the police would knock on Margaret's door. They would ask for a mouthful of soup and somewhere to sleep. Margaret was never afraid of these visits. She was used to them. During Napoleon's time, about seventy percent of young people avoided military conscription. They lived in small groups in the woods and on the mountains. They sometimes resorted to violence in order to survive.

There were also ex-soldiers who, after years of fighting, didn't want to go back to work, so they kept up their habit of taking up arms and robbing merchants as they returned from the markets. What was worrying was that not far behind the ex-soldiers there were often the police looking for them! But in the Bosco home there was a kind of tacit armistice. The police, tired out from climbing, would ask Margaret for a glass of water, and maybe even a glass of wine. The men, in the hayloft, would hear the voices and quietly run away. Don Lemoyne wrote, *Even though it was well known who was hiding in the house they would pretend not to know, and wouldn't attempt to arrest anyone.*

The Blind Man

There was a blind man living at The Becchi. Once he had been wealthy but he'd squandered it all. Now he lived in abject poverty. The youngsters gave him a wide berth. The mothers would point him out to their children and tell the story of the ant and the cicada, *While we were slaving away like ants, he would be singing away, having fun. He was as happy as a cicada. Now see what he has been reduced to. So learn something from it.* The old man was ashamed to beg, and he often went hungry. Margaret, at night, would leave a pot of steaming soup on the windowsill. The old man would come along in the dark and take it.

Mamma's White Bread

John was learning. He learned more about charity than saving. There was a boy working as a farmhand in a nearby farmhouse. His name was Secondo Matta. In the morning the master of the house would give him a slice of black bread and then hand him the halter for the two cows. His job was to take them off and pasture them until noon. Going down into the valley, he would meet up with John who was also taking his cows off to pasture, with a slice of white bread in his hands. In those days this kind of bread, known as *flour bread* was better quality, and cost much more than black bread. One day John said to him, *Do me a favour. I would like to swap bread with you. Yours tastes better than mine.* Secondo Matta believed him, and often they swapped bread. Only when he was an adult, he understood how kind John Bosco had been. When his nephew, Secondo Marchisio, became a Salesian priest, he asked him if he knew John Bosco. Secondo Matta told him about the time they swapped bread.

Death Returns

In February 1826, death visited the Bosco home once again. Eight years previously it had come to take his father. Now it was his parental grandmother, who departed. Don Lemoyne wrote, *around her beside, were Margaret and her grandchildren.* Grandmother, making an effort, said, *I am leaving for eternity. I recommend my soul to your prayers. Forgive me if sometimes I have been too severe, but it was for your good. Thank you, Margaret, for what you have done for me.* The she held her and kissed her with these words, *I am kissing you for the last time, but I hope to see all of you happy, in heaven.* Her grandchildren cried. Anthony, 18 years old, stared at her sorrowfully. With that old lady's death, the last blood link tying Anthony to his original family was broken. Grandmother gave up her soul on a cold winter's day in February. John Bosco, next to his mother saying the rosary with her children at the foot of grandma's bed, understood more clearly the words they repeated daily in the Hail Mary, *...now and at the hour of our death.* Don Bosco would see that his boys faced death bravely. He would call his monthly recollection *The Exercise for a Happy Death.*

First Communion Preparation

Forty-five days after his grandmother had died, it was Easter Sunday. On that day, John made his First Communion in the parish church at Castelnuovo. Here is how he recalls it:

> I was eleven years old when I received my First Communion. By now I knew all the catechism. Since the church was a long way away, I wasn't really known by the parish priest. I received all my religious instruction from my mother. She wanted me to carry out that great act of our faith as soon as possible. She prepared me well, doing everything she could. During Lent she sent me off to catechism classes every day.

John Filippello, a friend of John Bosco and the same age, went with him to the Lenten catechism classes held by the parish priest, Don Bartolomeo Dassano. He testified to the fact that occasionally the parish priest would shout at a student saying, *You hardly know any of your catechism, but Bosco not only knows how to recite it, he can sing it as well!*

Don Bosco continues:

> During Lent, my mother took me to confession three times. She would say to me each time, *John, God is giving you a great gift. Try to behave well, and make a sincere confession. Ask the Lord's forgiveness, and promise him you will be a good boy.* I promised. Whether or not I kept my promise, God only knows. On the evening before, she helped me to pray, made me read a good book, and gave me advice that only the truly Christian mother can think of giving her children.

> On the day of my First Communion, in the midst of that crowd of children and parents, it was almost impossible to remain recollected. My mother, in the morning, wouldn't let me go with anybody. She accompanied me to the altar. She made the preparation and thanksgiving with me. And she didn't want me involved in manual labour on that day. I spent my time reading and praying. She repeated the following words to me, *My son, this has been a wonderful day for you. I am certain God has become the Master of your heart. Promise him you will keep it that way all your life. From now on go to Communion often, but do not go with sin on your conscience. Always confess sincerely. Try always to be obedient. Go willingly to catechism class and listen to God's Word. But, for love of God, stay far away from bad company. Treat them like*

the plague. I always remembered and tried to carry out my mother's advice. From that day on I think I improved, at least a little.

From the words *God sees you,* said to her small son running around the yard, to the catechism she taught him so slowly and gently, Mamma Margaret gave her son a deep understanding of his faith. From her practical love for others to his first encounter with Jesus in the Eucharist, for which she prepared him so carefully, John learned *a sense of God.* Its magnificent fruits would be seen in John Bosco's personality.

10. Her Courage. His Courage

After the loss of her husband, Margaret did not retreat into anxiety and insecurity. In Don Bosco's memoirs we do not get the impression that he grew up hanging timidly on his mother's apron. He seems to have been a boy full of adventure and ready to take risks. Margaret was happy with this.

Her approach was, as much as possible, to reason things out with her children. With her neighbours, reasoning things out did not just mean taking it calmly, but discussing, at times even vigorously. The invitation, *We need to think about this,* meant, *Let's talk about it, discuss it, face up to it.* This is how the word *reason* became part of the life of John Bosco.

Lippa Spills Blood

One of John's most energetic pastimes was *Lippa*, a primitive kind of baseball. One afternoon John came back home, his face all covered in blood. The Lippa bat had smashed into his cheek. Margaret was concerned and while she was attending to the wound, said, *One day you're going to end up with a damaged eye. It would be better if you didn't go with those boys.* John replied, *If it will make you happy, I won't go with them. But look, Mamma, they are well behaved when I am with them. They don't say certain words.* Mamma Margaret thought about it, and then she let him go back to the game.

A Haunted Attic?

One autumn evening, while they were at supper with their grandparents in Capriglio, a loud noise came from the ceiling. It soon became a long drawn out screech; then a thud. They all looked up, holding their breath. One of the old ladies present began whispering about times past when they had heard noises coming from the attic, not just noises but groans and terrifying screams. *It was the devil. Now he's back,* she whispered, making the Sign of the Cross. John broke the silence, calmly suggesting, *I think it's a bird, not the devil. Mamma, let's go and see.* The women were wide-eyed. *Don't be crazy! Margaret, stop him! You don't play games with the devil.* John quietly turned to his mother, *You're not afraid, are you?* Margaret realised that she couldn't be, mustn't be, afraid. It was she who had taught him not to be afraid, had told him so many times that wizards and witches were just fables. She went up the wooden stairs after him. The rest of them clambered around, holding a lantern and offering a stick. As John pushed open the trapdoor to the attic, and held up the lantern to get a better look, a sack of cereal overturned, the contents began spilling out. The women cried out, but John calmly caught it and replaced it. A fat and rather ruffled chicken, imprisoned there, for who knows how long, ran away in fear. The others, laughing by this stage, gathered around John. The devil was a chicken, caught up while scavenging a few grains of wheat, then the sack had tipped on top of it, and it was dragging it around trying to get out!

The Nest

Bird's nests were John's passion. Among the hundred and one adventures in search of them, one went wrong for him. A tomtit's nest was deep down inside a broken tree trunk. He had thrust his arm down, up to the elbow, and then couldn't extract it. He tried and tried. Caught in the vice of the trunk's grip, his arm began to swell. Joseph ran to call their mother. Margaret arrived with a stepladder, but even she couldn't free his arm. She had to go off and find a farmer with a wedge and mallet. Joseph, more afraid than John, was yelling at him from down below, *Don't worry, they're coming!*

The farmer wrapped John's arm in his mother's apron then stuck the wedge in the crack along the tree trunk and began hitting it with the mallet. Seven or eight blows were sufficient. The crack widened, and his arm slipped out. Margaret didn't have the courage to reprimand him. She simply mumbled, *Don't get up to something like that again.*

Be Brave

Don Bosco instilled this same taste for adventure and lack of fear into his boys. He had learned from his mother to be brave and to admire those who were brave. Boys who gave in too easily, *still waters,* as he called them, he never regarded as *the best boys.* When he heard a mob of boys playing in Carmagnola's foggy streets one day, led by the authoritative voice of Michael Magone, Don Bosco straight away went to find the boy in charge. He brought Michael to Valdocco, because, as he said, he was a *boy who offers plenty of hope, even if he's a bit of a troublemaker.* He always thought highly of anyone who was brave enough to take risks.

Throughout his life, Don Bosco was always courageous: from the founding of the Oratory, despite enormous difficulties, to the founding of the Salesian Congregation at a time when secular forces were seeking to suppress religious congregations. He would encourage his youngsters to acts of bravery that today would be regarded as sheer foolishness. In 1854 he invited the older boys to come with him to visit the homes of cholera sufferers, to look after those who were sick. Courage was another fundamental lesson learned from his mother.

11. The Great Dream

Mamma Margaret did not educate her sons just by word and example. She was aware of what was special about each of them, their growing temperament, their various strengths. These original and special features she respected and sought to direct for the best. In Don Lemoyne's *Life of Mamma Margaret*, personally reviewed by Don Bosco, the biographer writes, *Margaret watched her sons' behaviour carefully, and prayed to the Lord that she could discern the path each was to take.* In John's life, something extraordinary was about to happen. He himself tells us about it:

It was when I was nine that I had a dream, which remained deeply impressed on my mind all my life. In this dream I found myself in a fairly large yard. A crowd of children were playing there. Some were laughing, some were playing games, and quite a few were swearing. When I heard these evil words, I jumped amongst them immediately and tried to stop them by shouting at them and waving my fists. At that moment a dignified man appeared, nobly dressed. He wore a white cloak, and his face shone. I could not look directly at him. He called me by name and told me to take charge of these children, and added these words, *You will have to win these friends of yours not by blows but by gentleness and love. Start right away to teach them the ugliness of sin and the value of virtue.*

Confused and frightened, I replied that I was a poor ignorant child, unable to talk to those youngsters about religion. At that moment the young people stopped their laughing, shouting and swearing; they gathered around the man who was speaking. Hardly knowing what I was saying, I asked, *Who are you, ordering me to do the impossible?* The man replied, *Precisely because it seems impossible to you, you must make it possible through obedience and acquisition of knowledge.*

Where, by what means, can I acquire knowledge?

I will give you a teacher. Under her guidance you can become wise. Without her, all wisdom is foolish.

But who are you?

I am the son of the woman whom your mother has taught you to greet three times a day.

My mother tells me to avoid strangers. I need her permission. So tell me your name.

Ask my mother what my name is.

At that moment I saw a lady of stately appearance standing beside him. She was wearing a mantle that sparkled all over as though covered with bright stars. Seeing from my questions and answers that I was more confused than ever, she beckoned me to approach her. She took me kindly by the hand and said, *Look*. Glancing around, it seemed that the youngsters had all run away. A large number of goats, dogs, cats, bears and other animals had taken their place. The stately lady said, *This is the field of your work. Make yourself humble, strong and energetic. And what you will see happening to these animals in a moment is what you must do for my children.*

I looked around again, and where before I had seen wild animals, I now saw gentle lambs. They were all gambolling and bleating as if to welcome that man and lady. At that moment, still dreaming, I began to cry. I begged the lady to speak so that I could understand her, because I did not know what all this could mean. Then she placed her hand on my head and said *In time, you will understand everything.*

With that, a noise woke me up. Everything had disappeared. I was totally bewildered. My hands seemed to be sore from the blows I had given, and my face hurt from those I had received.

In the morning I immediately told the dream, first to my brothers who laughed at the whole thing, then to my mother and grandmother. Each gave their own interpretation. Joseph said, *You're going to become a keeper of goats, sheep and other animals.* My mother commented *Who knows, but you may become a priest.* Anthony merely grunted, *Perhaps you'll become a bandit.* But my grandmother, though she could not read or write, knew enough theology and made the final judgment, saying, *Pay no attention to dreams.* I agreed with my grandmother. However, I was unable to cast that dream out of my mind.[7]

Mamma Margaret's New Approach

This dream was the first time the extraordinary broke into John Bosco's life. The upbringing received from his mother was now complemented by this event. God's call had come, guiding and advising. *The dream at nine years of age*, writes Peter Stella,[8] *changed Don Bosco's entire way of looking at and thinking about things. It also altered Mamma Margaret's approach. For her too, it was a manifestation of a higher will, a clear sign of her son's priestly vocation.*[9] Margaret was prepared to put up with all kinds of humiliations and difficulties to help her son to become a priest.

---

[7] Memoirs, pp. 18-20

[8] One of the most qualified researchers on Don Bosco

[9] Stella I, 30-31

12. Margaret finds a school for John

It was John's dream to become a priest and to help youngsters. But there was a difficult road ahead to make it a reality; long years of schooling. John wanted to go to school, and Mamma Margaret also wanted him to go. Margaret had never needed, as a mother, to persuade her son to study! But there were major difficulties.

The law in the Kingdom of Piedmont had ordered all counties to provide a free basic primary school, with a two-year curriculum. But the county to which that forgotten little hamlet of The Becchi belonged was Castelnuovo, five kilometres away. It would be impossible for a nine-year-old to go there on foot every day. The child would need to find a good family to board with in Castelnuovo, and return home only on Saturday afternoon.

This was when the real difficulties began. His brother Anthony didn't want to hear about it, absolutely not! He himself had only gone to school for a few months, he could sign documents with his own name and surname, but he had left school behind as a joke. *It's all stories! Learn to write your signature, but you need work to earn your living, not school!* Eighteen-year-old Anthony worked hard. It was his work that earned the family a decent livelihood. He didn't want any of his money wasted sending his young brother to school. Margaret was used to Anthony's temperament by now, but she did not dare contradict him.

Don Bevilacqua

Like all intelligent and curious children, John taught himself to read. Michael Rua tells us, *The young Bosco had a kind farmer as the first one to teach him to read. Years later, this man told me he was so proud he had been lucky enough to be his teacher.* This occurred somewhere between 1823 and 1824.

Then came a stroke of good luck. An elderly farmer, John Bechis, known as *Vanin,* tells the story:

> In Capriglio a certain Don Bevilacqua[10] was the local priest. He ran the primary school there. Mamma Margaret, not wanting to send her boy to Castelnuovo because he was too young, begged Don Bevilacqua to admit him to his school. Margaret had been born in Capriglio. She had been married in the Capriglio Church. Her father, Melchior, and her brothers and sisters still lived there. Since he was obliged only to admit children from Capriglio, the

---

[10] Surnames, in those days, were not always accurate. The priest-teacher is registered in the town as *Joseph Lacqu'*, while Vanin calls him *Bevilacqua*, and Don Bosco in his Memoirs, calls him *Dellacqua*.

priest did not want to take John. Then his housekeeper died. Her place was taken by John's aunt, Marianna, Margaret's sister. She immediately asked the priest to admit her nephew to the school. He agreed, and John Bosco attended his school.

Margaret then went with John to grandfather Melchior's place, and for three hours each morning, (three and a half, if one counts the obligatory Mass for all students), and another three hours each afternoon, he learned *reading, writing and arithmetic*. He had lunch with his Aunt Marianna. The school year was not so long. It began on November 3rd, after the feast of All Saints and All Souls, and finished on March 24th, vigil of the Annunciation. By 1826 John had completed the first two classes.

Three Books Borrowed

Don Bevilacqua became quite fond of the small farming boy from The Becchi, who was so keen to read and study. Later Don Bosco wrote:

> My teacher was a devout priest, very attentive to my needs, seeing to my instruction and even more to my Christian education.

Seeing that he was so keen to read, the priest lent him three adventure stories before the long holidays began: *Wretched Guerino, The Kings of France* and *Bertoldo and Bertoldino.* Mamma Margaret, when she saw John come back with three big books, smiled and thought: *How can a child read all these?* She soon changed her mind, because after a couple of weeks John had devoured them. Of an evening, by the faint light of the oil lamp, he began reading them to Joseph and some of his friends who were entranced by those pages full of wondrous adventures.

13. With a Mother's Encouragement

Word quickly spread that John Bosco, who was only eleven years old, was reading marvellous stories to his friends. Don Bosco writes:

> When I appeared, my companions would run to me in a crowd. They loved to spend an evening listening spellbound to a reading from *The Kings of France*. Before and after the reading we would make the Sign of the Cross and say a Hail Mary. This was 1826.

In the dream when he was nine, John had seen a throng of boys, and he had been told to do good to them. Almost without realising it, he had begun to do just that. The marvellous adventures of the Emperor Charles the Great and his knights, the epic sword fights of Durlindana and Gano's perfidious betrayals, were a great success, and attracted a crowd of youngsters around him who followed him like a little leader. When reading these adventure stories he would always add, *Now let us say a little prayer.*

Margaret Approves

With the arrival of summer, John had a new surprise for his young spectators. On fair days and market days he had gone to watch the magicians and acrobats. He had carefully observed their magic tricks, their sleight of hand. Back home, he practised over and over again until, after lots of spills and falls, he could do the same tricks. Later he wrote:

> Would you believe it, but by the time I was eleven I could juggle, do mid-air somersaults and the swallow trick and walk on my hands. I could walk, jump and even dance on the tightrope like a professional acrobat.

On feast days, the local boys and some from far away would come looking for him. He would announce the show. Then he would invite them to say the rosary and sing a hymn. Then jumping up on a chair he would repeat the sermon he had heard at Mass that morning. Finally the show would begin: somersaults, all kinds of twists and turns, magic, and tightrope walking. At the end, totally exhausted, he would finish the show with a short prayer.

In his memoirs Don Bosco wrote:

> Now you might ask me: did my mother mind my wasting my time playing the magician? My mother loved me dearly, and I had boundless trust in her. I would not take one step without her approval. She knew everything, saw everything and let me do it. Indeed, if I needed something she willingly came to my help.

At times Margaret came to watch John, together with a neighbour, Catherine Agagliati, who was most enthusiastic about what she saw and heard. At one point Margaret asked her: *What do you think my son will become?* Catherine answered: *He is certainly going to make an impression on the world!* Don Lemoyne, later commented, *Don Bosco, who was already getting on in years, was laughing when he told me this.*

Margaret's Difficult Son

But there was someone else watching everything too, Anthony. He was strong as a bull, and suspicious. As he watched John, his anger grew. Sometimes at table there would be an outburst, *Here am I breaking my back in the fields, while this one here is playing magician! No good will come of this.* John would shrug his shoulders. Margaret instead would suffer in silence. Anthony was seven years older than John, and had become rather introspective, rough and coarse. He would sometimes push his younger brothers around, and Margaret would have to come and rescue them. He was a hypersensitive boy; the death of both his parents had traumatised him.

His attitude to Margaret alternated between tenderness and anger. At times, when he was reprimanded for his behaviour, he would raise his hands to her, and shout, *Stepmother!* Margaret could have physically put him in his place; other mothers in those days had few scruples about doing so, but she found that sort of treatment pointless. She never once raised a hand to him, but she dealt with him firmly, *Anthony, I am your mother, not your stepmother. Now calm down and think about it. You will see that you are in the wrong.* John found these scenes frightening, but he was learning from his mother how to deal with anger.

14. Leaving Home

The young lad, John, enjoyed sitting at the table on long winter evenings or by the fireplace. It was for him a time of peace and security. Margaret, despite her husband's death and Anthony's moods, and her heavy workload, knew how to make these evenings a time of *family warmth* for her boys. John loved these moments. For the rest of his life he would often recall these halcyon days. It all came to a sudden end in February 1827. He was not yet twelve but, because of Anthony's anger, he was forced to flee the family nest.

Margaret Watches John Leave

One evening, at table, Anthony saw that John had a book open, next to his plate. He exploded, *I'm going to throw that book into the fire!* Margaret calmly said, *John does as much work as the others. If he likes reading, what's that got to do with you?* Anthony retaliated; *It's got everything to do with me because I'm the only one keeping this hovel from falling around our ears. It's me who's breaking his back on the land. I have no intention of letting some little lord enjoy himself while the rest of us are left eating polenta.*

John began to argue with him; he was never short of a word. Anthony raised his hand. Margaret tried to put herself between them, but John took a beating. In bed John cried, more from anger than pain, while Margaret cried next door. That night she couldn't sleep, and finally came to a momentous decision. In the morning she said the saddest words John had ever heard, *It would be better for you to leave home. One day Anthony is going to really hurt you.* John could only say, *Where will I go?* In anguish, Margaret pointed out the road to the Moglia farm in Moncucco, the lady of the house, Dorothy Filipello was her friend. John went off into the fog. In the bag slung over his shoulder were a couple of shirts, some bread rolls, and his books.

The Moglias did not find it so easy to take him in. Louis, the head of the house said to him, *But my poor boy, it's winter, we don't take on stable hands until March. Besides you are so small.* John felt so helpless and tired. He broke into tears, *Please take me in, for charity's sake. No need to pay me, but please don't send me back home.* Dorothy took pity on him, *Let's take him in. Let's try it at least for a few days.* So began John's life as a stable hand. He remained there nearly three years, during which time he grew into a man, but in silence he often cried the tears of a boy, far from his family. His mother cried quietly, back in her cottage at The Becchi.

Don Bosco, when speaking of his Salesian communities, would often use the word *Family*. For his entire life he worked to see that his boys, many of them orphans without a home, were offered the kindness, peace and security of a family.

Margaret Visits John

Despite the separation, which lasted about three years, Margaret did not abandon her son. She followed his progress from a distance, waiting for the right moment to bring him back home and enable him to continue the studies that would take him towards the priesthood.

That opportunity came on February 3rd 1829. Anthony, turned twenty-one, became an adult. That was when Margaret was able to set in motion proceedings to divide the family heritage up between Anthony and his brothers, finally making the way clear for John to continue his studies.

Louis Moglia, an honest man, wanted to draw up a proper work contract between himself and the boy's mother. George Moglia, Louis' son, then just three at the time, later recounted what he had heard from his parents:

> Eight days after John's arrival, my family formally took on young John Bosco to look after him and clothe him until the end of the season They were satisfied with his work, and gave his mother thirty lire, and the following year, fifty lire. I had a chance to see the obedience and respect John showed his mother, especially on feast days when we would invite her to the hamlet to stay with us.

Our Lady Our Mother

Amongst the experiences young John Bosco had at the Moglia farm, there is one event which throws light on the spiritual dimension of the education given him by his mother. One day, old Joseph, the Moglia's uncle, came back from the fields all covered in perspiration and with his hoe over his shoulders. It was midday, and the Moncucco bell was ringing out the *Angelus*. The old man, tired out, sat down on some hay to regain his breath. Not far away he saw John, also on the hay but kneeling. He was saying the *Angelus*, the prayer his mother had taught him to say three times a day, the prayer that reminds us that the Son of God, through Our Lady's *Yes* to the angel, was made man and dwelt amongst us. Joseph complained: *We farmers are working while the farm hands are praying!* John, the prayer over, answered with a grin: *When there is work to be done, Joseph, you know I'm always there. My mother taught me that when we pray, two grains produce four; if we don't pray, four grains will only produce two. So you'd be better off praying.*

Margaret, by example, more than by words, had taught John that Our Lady was a *mother for every day*. John learned to hoe, mow the grass, handle the clippers and milk the cows. A true farmer moving barefoot from field to field, and by night going to bed on a mattress stuffed with corn leaves. For him, as for Margaret, Our Lady, the Madonna, was an every-day mother, one he met *in the morning* when the cock crew and it was time to overcome sleep and laziness because there was much work to be done during the day; *at noon* during the break the farmer takes, sitting on the grass, munching happily on bread and pulling the cork from the bottle; *in the evening,* when tiredness weighs heavily, and the return home brings the simple joy of being home, around the blazing fire, with one's dear ones around the table.

This was the basic love for Our Lady that John Bosco naturally gained from his mother Margaret, and which later Don Bosco would hand on to his boys and to his Salesians. Our Lady is mother to her children while they work, pray, and journey towards heaven. *Devotion to Our Lady* is that homely, familiar encounter with our mother each day.

I Must be a Priest

As the months passed, during those regular meetings with his mother, John often asked: *When can I recommence my studies?* For the first time in his life he began to say openly: *I will be a priest.* During the hot summer days, while the animals were peacefully chewing under the trees, John, whose job it was to keep an eye on them, would find some time for his books. Louis Moglia asked him one day, *Why do you do so much reading?* John replied, *Because I want to become a priest.*

Sometimes, in the yard, Anna, one of the Moglia's little girls, would come along. She was tired of being alone, and wanted to play with someone. But John often wouldn't notice her, so absorbed was he in his book. Anna would pull a long face: *Why won't you play with me?* John would smile at her, *I must become a priest, so I have to study.* The child, annoyed, would toss her head, *That's not true. You will be a cowherd like Joseph!* One day John said to her in all seriousness, *I really will be a priest one day, and you will come to confession to me.*

Many years later Anna married Joseph Zucca, became a mother, and went to the Oratory in Valdocco on various occasions to greet Mamma Margaret and to go to confession to Don Bosco and attend his Mass. Don Bosco happily welcomed her like a sister.

15. An End to Exile

In November 1829 the splitting up of the inheritance with Anthony had not yet been completed. The Town Council had explained to Margaret that the brothers, Joseph and John, with whom Anthony would need to share the inheritance, were minors. And unless Anthony agreed, it could not be done. Anthony had no desire to do anything about it. It would mean losing his position as head of the family, which he found to be convenient for the moment. In fact he was thinking of getting married shortly.

Michael Occhiena, Margaret's younger brother, and John's uncle therefore, went to the Moglia farm to speak with John. He wanted to see if John would be prepared to stay a little longer at the farm. He found him letting the cows out.
So, John, are you happy to stay here?
No. They look after me very well, but I want to study. The years are moving on, I've already turned 14 and I'm at a standstill, not going anywhere.
Well, just put the cows back into the stall and come back to The Becchi. I will speak with the two who are in charge, then I have to go to the Chieri market. But this evening I am going to your place and we will arrange everything.

Michael was one who acted on impulse, with the strength of his thirty-four years and the indignation of an uncle who saw that his nephew was humiliated and his sister mortified by someone upsetting the family who was, in reality, merely a half-brother. If someone needed to tackle the twenty-one-year-old Anthony, he would do it. He had worked *gratis* for two years to pay Margaret's dowry to Francis Bosco, had worked solidly to ensure the shack left by Francis was habitable, and had given a hand to Margaret, Francis' widow, whenever she needed it. And now one of Francis' sons was in control in his sister's home!

Leaving the Moglia Family

John took up his bag again, said farewell to Dorothy, Stephen, Joseph, Teresa, Anna and little George. They had become friends and would remain so for the rest of their lives. He set back out on the road to The Becchi. Mamma Margaret saw him from way off and ran to meet him: *Anthony is still at home. Don't let him see you until Uncle Michael arrives. If Anthony sees you he will suspect something, and God only knows what will happen.* Mamma Margaret was concerned that John's sudden appearance would make Anthony suspect some plot to force him to share the inheritance. His uncle arrived that evening. Anthony's handshake was cold as he welcomed him to the house. There followed a tense discussion, but not war.

Anthony received a guarantee that the inheritance would not be touched until he was married, and that John's studies and upkeep, now that he was back home, would not be down to him. Grudgingly he accepted.

Uncle Michael used to provide the wine for the seminary in Chieri, and he had many friends amongst the surrounding parish clergy. He assured Margaret that he would have no difficulty finding John a place at school in Chieri. While he was making arrangements with the parish priests of Castelnuovo and Buttigliera, he encountered some unexpected difficulties. Meanwhile John's circumstances changed.

Don Calosso

That November there was a *mission*, in Buttigliera, a village not far from The Becchi. Many went to hear the renowned priest who was preaching the mission. John also went along. Coming home in the evening he mingled with the other people who came from Morialdo and from The Becchi. With the parishioners from Morialdo there was also an elderly priest, over seventy years of age. A few months before he had agreed to be chaplain in Morialdo. He was stooped as he walked. His name was John Melchior Calosso, he had a degree in theology and had been parish priest in Bruino for a long time. He noticed the curly-headed youngster whom he hadn't seen before. John had only just come back from the Moglia farm.

In 1863, Dominic Ruffino, a young Salesian,[11] together with other Salesians decided to make daily notes of whatever Don Bosco said. The result was a diary written in a hurry late at night. Its language is not perfect, but fresh and to the point. As Dominic says, *These were things we heard from Don Bosco himself, things he told us during recreation.* We should regard them, therefore, as Don Bosco's reminiscences, rather than an autobiography. He talked about his meeting with Don Calosso as follows:

> I had attended the mission. Coming back from the church I came across Don Calosso, the Murialdo chaplain, who must have thought I was a rascal,[12] which I was, bare-headed and unkempt, running through every puddle. He called me over:
> *Which village are you from?*
> *I'm from The Becchi.*
> *Where are you coming from?*
> *From listening to the sermon.*
> *Oh, did you understand anything of it?*
> *I understood it all.*

---

[11] Don Bosco was 48 and Ruffino 23

[12] *Rascason*

If you are bright enough to tell me three points from it I will give you three coins.
Which one do you want to hear about, the first or the second?
Tell me about the second one.
All of it or just part of it?
Three words will do.
If you just want three quotes I can give them to you immediately.
I started to recall the sermon:
The encounter between body and soul when it is time for the two to be united before the final judgment will be a shock.
I went on like that for about ten minutes; Don Calosso stared at me, along with everyone else there; then he said,
Come and find me at home, I have something I want to say to you.
Then he left me.
I went to the chaplain's house, where he said to me,
I need to write those sermons down. Do you think you could let me hear some more of them?
Yes, but I don't know all the exact Italian words.
That doesn't matter.
So I repeated an entire sermon. The priest was impressed by my memory. Finally he said to me
Could you ask your mother to drop in; I would like to speak to her.
My mother called in and he said to her,
Were you aware that your son has a prodigious memory? You need to get him to study.
My mother replied, *I would be very happy but his brother absolutely forbids it.*
Not to worry, send him here and I will teach him.
The following day I started; but my brother was in a terrible mood. He wanted me to work instead. Don Calosso had given me his Donato.[13] At first I found some difficulty with the first declension and the first verb. It soon became easy, reading and studying. After twenty-eight days I knew the book off by heart. The priest said:
If you carry on like this you will soon know everything there is to know in the world.
Meanwhile, at home, there were always problems. When I explained this to Don Calosso he said;
If that's the way it is, then bring some clothes and stay here. Know for sure that I will not abandon you.
My mother was not happy about my going, but there was no other way.

---

[13] Latin grammar of the time

Margaret Sends John to His Grandfather

November 21st 1830, a year after he started studying with Don Calosso, was a very sad day for John. The priest, who had been so kind to him, died of apoplexy, after two days in agony. Mamma Margaret tried to comfort him, but she saw that there was nothing she could do to make up for the loss of his teacher, his friend.

Before he died, the chaplain had given him a guarantee that *while I am alive you will lack for nothing; if I die, I will provide for you.* He gave him to understand that the 6000 lire he received for his stipend would go towards John's schooling. It was a huge sum if you consider that a pair of oxen were worth 200 lire, and a farm hand would earn only one lira a day. But when the priest's family arrived and began talking about their inheritance, John had no idea that a quarrel was about to break out around the mortal remains of his *guardian angel*. He writes in his memoirs: *Along with him, every hope of mine died too,* for he goes on to write, *The family arrived, and I handed over to them the key and everything else.* His mother was standing nearby. *Fearing for my sanity, she sent me for a while to my grandfather's in Capriglio.*[14]

---

[14] Memoirs of the Oratory p 43

16. Walking to Castelnuovo

1830, which had begun so wonderfully, ended so miserably. It finished with the dividing up of the inheritance. The small house, too, was divided up. Anthony had everything facing east, including the largest room, the stable, the woodpile and the ladder. Joseph and John, with their mother as guarantor because they were still minors, were given the kitchen, the room where he had his dream at nine years of age, the hayloft and the porch. Anthony went to live in his part of the house, on his own. Not for long, though. Some months after, on March 22nd, 1831, he married a fine young woman from Castelnuovo, Anna Rosso, and went to work for another farmer in order to have a more secure future. Mamma Margaret endured these events with courage, but also a touch of sadness.

During the growing season of 1830-31 she lived with Joseph who was now seventeen and John who was fifteen at The Becchi. They cultivated their small plot and lived in the half of the house they had gained when the inheritance was divided.

After Christmas 1830, having spoken at length with his mother and brother, John began to attend school in Castelnuovo. His thirst for study ensured that the ten kilometres each day felt like a normal walk. Mamma Margaret prepared a bread roll for lunch, and he put it in the little bag he swung over his shoulders, along with his books. A witness to those journeys tells us, *To save what he could for his poor mother, as soon as he left home he took off his shoes, and only put them back on as he climbed up to Castelnuovo.* The poverty of the Bosco home, even though Mamma Margaret managed things well, meant they lived on the edge of survival.

A Cold February

It was winter when John began his daily walk to school. Among the Monferrato hills, January is usually cool but sunny. The really bad weather arrives in February, with snowfalls and ice. Ten kilometres a day in that kind of climate was bound to affect one's health. Mamma Margaret, who kept a good eye on John, decided to call a halt to the daily trudges to Castelnuovo. She went to Castelnuovo with him, and there she arranged modest but safe lodgings for him.

> I was boarding with a good man called John Roberto, a tailor by profession. He had a taste for singing, especially plainchant. Since I had a good voice, I took up music wholeheartedly. In a few months I could take the stage to accompany him with fair success. Eager to use my free time, I took up tailoring. Before long I was able to make buttonholes, and hems, and sew simple and double seams. I like to think I became a master-tailor. My landlord,

seeing how I had taken to the trade, offered me a job. I had other ambitions, however: I wanted to pursue my studies.[15]

Each week Mamma Margaret came along to see how things were going. She kept an eye on the progress John was making in his studies and made contact with his teachers. She would bring him some provisions and bread to last the week, and for John Roberto the rent, which consisted of some cereal and a few litres of wine.

At the beginning, his studies were not going too well. *The studies I had done privately,* Don Bosco recalls, *were not so helpful for going to a public school with new teachers. I almost had to start over again with the Italian grammar in order to take up Latin.* Besides, the eleven-year-old boys from Castelnuovo laughed at the gangly fifteen-year-old country boy with his wooden clogs. Their ringleader used to whisper rather loudly, *He smells like a goat.*

But the teacher, Don Emmanuel Virano, warmly accepted this boy, who was making such an effort to continue his studies. He gave him extra lessons, and in no time brought him up to the level of the others. When Mamma Margaret would ask about his studies, he said: *Everything is going well, Signora. No need to worry.*

In April 1831, Don Emmanuel was chosen to be parish priest of Mondonio, and needed to get another teacher to replace him. Don Nicholas came along, worn out and elderly, and soon lost control of the class. Don Bosco writes sadly, *Unable to keep order, he almost scattered to the winds all I had learned in the previous months.*

John spoke about this problem with his mother. At times, Don Nicholas took it out on him, thinking that, because of his size, he had to be the cause of the disturbances. With all the noise in the classroom and Don Nicholas' shouting, it meant he was wasting time. With his mother's agreement, he went to work for some hours each day with Evasio Savio, a blacksmith. He learned to use the hammer and tongs, and work the forge. The rest of the day he spent working with John Roberto. In this way he earned some money. He was soon going to need this because, with Mamma Margaret's encouragement, he had made the decision to try, that autumn, to apply for some serious schooling in Chieri.

---

[15] Memoirs of the Oratory. p 49

17. The Road to Chieri

By autumn 1831, Joseph was a lively eighteen-year-old. Coming to an understanding with his mother and brother, he decided to leave The Becchi. With a friend, Joseph Febbraro, the Matta family had employed him as a tenant-farmer in Sussambrino. This consisted of a well-built house with some vineyards, which ran along the road between The Becchi and Castelnuovo.

Somewhere around November 11th, the Feast of Saint Martin, the move took place. Mamma Margaret left the patched up old cottage with just a touch of sadness. This was where her husband had died. She returned occasionally, so as not to leave the land untended nor abandon the handful of rooms to the elements.

John, once at Sussambrino with his mother and brother, kept going over the calculations of costs involved in taking up schooling in Chieri. In this city, fifteen kilometres from Castelnuovo and ten from Turin, the public schools, called *colleges* were held in high esteem. In fact they were classified as *affiliated to the University of Turin*.

For the second time John had to begin again. He would need to enrol in the first preparatory class, and during that scholastic year 1831-32 he would have to try to cover the second preparatory class and, if possible, the *first latinità, or classical year*. Then there was the second and third *latinità*, and finally *humanities* and *rhetoric* to complete.

Begging for Help

As well as the difficulties in his studies, John had to resolve the financial problems too. Each year he would need to pay the school fees[16] of 12 lire, buy his books and find the cheapest place to rent (about 21 lire a month). To have a rough estimate of how this compares to today's figures, it is enough to consider that a Chieri silk worker earned two lire a day, while a woman doing the same work would only earn 60 to 80 cents a day.

Don Secondo Marchisio, immediately after Don Bosco's death, went around the hills in Morialdo and Castelnuovo to collect memories of Don Bosco's youth. On page seven of his dossier he wrote:

> While Mamma Margaret was preparing the necessary funding, along with other things needed to send her child off to study, John Bosco was aware

---

[16] Minervale

that his mother was in difficult straits. One day he said to her, *if you are happy about it I will go around every family in the hamlet to make a collection.* Margaret Bosco agreed and John went from door to door asking for charity; something to help to pay for him to go to Chieri to study. He was given bread, fruit, melica,[17] cheeses and eleven emina[18] of cereal. Some also gave him money. A certain John Becchis, unable to give him anything, agreed to take whatever was collected to Chieri.

A good woman from The Becchi, who at that time had to go to Castelnuovo, went to the parish priest Don Dassano. She told him, in no uncertain terms, that the parish priest should be the first to offer help to a good young man going off to study for the priesthood, he shouldn't need to go begging for help. Don Dassano had known nothing about his plight, so he made some enquiries. He then he took up a collection himself and gave it to Margaret. He also suggested that she speak to Lucia Matta, a widow who was staying in Chieri.

Lucia had decided to stay near her own son in Chieri, because he was reluctant to study. Margaret asked if John could stay with her. The rent would still be 21 lire, but Margaret was allowed to pay, in part, with flour and wine. John also agreed to help Lucia's son in his studies and do the housework, from cutting wood for the stove, to putting out the washing.

Don Secondo Marchisio, on page seven of his dossier, continues:
> John Filipello, also known as Balada, was fourteen when he met Margaret Bosco with John when they went to Chieri. Margaret, taken up with domestic matters at home, begged Filipello to go to Chieri with John who was going there to study: to go fifteen kilometres, on foot, along those country roads, with money in your pocket, was dangerous. Filipello agreed and with some money as recompense from Margaret, went off to Chieri with John.

On page nine of the dossier he adds:
> For a monthly rent of 21 lire, he went to Chieri to study, living in the house owned by a certain Lucia Matta. He stayed with her for two years, but because he was so well behaved she asked for no rent from him, leaving him to buy his books and some clothing with the money.

At noon, when John and his friend Filipello arrived, Mamma Margaret also turned up at Chieri. She went to Lucia Matta's house. There Margaret presented her son

---

[17] Sorghum - a cereal crop

[18] One emina=a quarter of a litre

and gave her the first sacks of grain that John Becchis had brought along with the collection. *This is my son,* she said, *here is the first part of the rent. I have done my part, my son will now do his. I hope you will not be unhappy with him.* Margaret was pleased with the arrangement, but she had difficulty hiding her tears as she left to return to the farm in Sussambrino.

18. Margaret a Grandmother

Chieri lies on a hill outside Turin; at that time it had a population of nine thousand. Many were students attending schools; others were textile workers, in the thirty or so textile factories, weaving the precious and well known Chieri brocades, an elaborately woven cloth. The students from Asti and the Monferrato region had to work hard to make ends meet. Many like John found work, from giving private lessons to other students to cleaning homes or stables. Although Mamma Margaret sent him some food, John often went hungry in those first weeks. He did get some food from one of his friends, Joseph Blanchard, whose mother sold bread and fruit. But despite some difficult times, the years from 1831 to 1835 were for John a time when his rich personality developed rapidly. These years from 16 to 20 years of age, were the prime of his life.

Peter Stella tells us:

It was life without frustrations. In fact it was a euphoric time, partly because of his scholastic success, but also because of the respect given him by school friends, who appreciated his company. He had graduated in Chieri within a few months.

And also, in just one year, he completed his second and third courses with outstanding results. In 1834-35 he finished his Humanities year just as brilliantly, and went on to Rhetoric the following year. The teachers helped him, and each year his excellent results meant he was soon dispensed from school fees.

These were the years we see deep friendships develop around him. He founded the *Società dell'Allegria,*[19] which showed the way to great challenges and exciting adventures. This is where Louis Comollo and the Jewish boy, Jonah became his close friends.

One Mother to Another

Margaret travelled every fortnight from Sussambrino to Chieri, bringing a basket of bread and focaccia[20] for John, and whatever was required for the rent for Lucia Matta. She would ask about her son, as one mother to another. Lucia would often complain to Margaret, *If only my son was like yours. He's lazy, disobedient and his results are poor. John, who is younger than he is, does help him with his homework. You*

---

[19] It defies an appropriate English translation; *The Society of Joy* does not do it justice

[20] Italian bread made with herbs and olive oil

are so lucky, Margaret, to have a son like that. After two years, Lucia Matta moved away from Chieri. John Bosco then had to find somewhere else to rent. Mamma Margaret came from Sussambrino to give him a hand, and spoke to different people she knew, but it proved difficult to find a place.

On May 10th 1889, Don John Baptist Francesia went to Chieri to find out something about Don Bosco's youth. He met a man called Joseph Pianta, who, though quite old, remembered the young John Bosco:

> Don Bosco's mother begged me to take him in at my place. I was managing an inn at the time. I gave him somewhere to stay and some soup, provided he did some housework. His mother used to supply him with bread and food she had cooked. Once he had done the housework and recorded the scores on the billiard table, he would study and read. He showed great tact in dealing with those who used bad language in the bar. You couldn't find a better worker!

Although he appreciated his help, Pianta could only offer him a place under the stairwell, as a bedroom. It seemed like a prison cell, but John didn't complain.

Despite the sacrifices he made, he thrived on the chance to study, on the opportunity for prayer, on the company of like-minded young men, and the friendships made with people like Louis Comollo. The human and Christian upbringing he had gained began to flourish to its fullest; upbringing experienced from Mamma Margaret in the cheerful life and painful sacrifices of The Becchi, the Moglia experience, the roads he had trodden with his bag of books slung over his shoulder, as well as his shoes, to wear them out as little as possible. All of this had accustomed him to a faith lived in joy and sacrifice, without compromise and without any fear of being a witness and an apostle.

Peaceful Years in Sussambrino

Mamma Margaret spent from 1831 to 1836 in the big house at Sussambrino. For her, these were *peaceful years*. Joseph and his friend Febbraro did well on the farm through hard work, giving her the freedom to attend to the less demanding tasks around the house, looking after the chickens and the rabbits.

On March 9th, 1833 Joseph, who was now 20 years old, married Mary Calosso. A year later, Margaret held her first grandchild, Anna, in her arms. At 46 she had become a grandmother. Other grandchildren followed: Philomena, Rosa Domenica, Francis and Louis. She was the happiest grandmother in the world. But she still lived in poverty. Many children meant many mouths to feed. The farmer's life, while the children are small, is a constant effort to ensure there is enough bread and soup.

For Margaret there was the matter of John's poverty too. Her thoughts went to her son who was so different from the others, to his new and unknown life as a student. She tried to save so that every fortnight she could take him some bread and money for his books, which were so costly then, and were sold and resold from student to student. She knew the money was not enough, and that John supplemented it by helping other students and doing different jobs to make ends meet.

When she sat in the shade and had no more beans to strip, she fingered the rosary, which she always carried in the pocket of her apron, with her keys and a crust of bread. That rosary gave her a sense of security.

19. John Bosco a Monk?

For John, too, concern about finance, about being the least burden possible to his mother, was a constant worry. With the help he gave to Lucia's son with his studies and the menial jobs he did, he managed to pay the rent. From Pianta he accepted whatever work was on offer, for it pained him to ask his mother for money.

In April 1834, he would be nineteen and would finish his *Humanities* year. It was time to decide what to do in life. With the studies he had completed he could be a lawyer's clerk or work in a notary's office. He could get his qualification to teach in the primary school, or could get work in the Council offices.

He writes in his memoirs:

> The dream I had in Murialdo was deeply imprinted on my mind; in fact it had recurred several times more in ever-clearer terms, so that if I wanted to have faith in it I would have to pursue the priesthood, towards which I actually felt inclined.

To become a priest he needed another year of public school, *Rhetoric*, then he needed to enter the seminary and complete another six years of study at a higher level. Although these studies were demanding, he felt he could cope, but they would also be expensive and he wasn't sure he could manage. He couldn't bear the thought of telling his mother, who was now nearly fifty, and still counting every penny, *Keep me for another seven years*.

In the final days of April, after thinking about it for a long time, he walked to Castelnuovo, presented himself to his parish priest, Don Dassano, and asked him for the documents needed to enter the Franciscans in Chieri. The parish priest was shocked, *John Bosco in a monastery? But have you given this proper thought? Have you spoken to your mother about it?* John told him everything he had been thinking about, he couldn't face up to the cost of another seven years of study. The monthly fees would be higher, his mother was no longer young, his brother had a child to support, and there would soon be other children. He also said he had spoken with some of the Franciscan priests in Chieri. They would willingly take him, he could finish his studies without worry and then become a Franciscan priest. From the moment he entered the monastery his education would be free.

Don Dassano's Advice

Don Dassano understood his arguments, but he could appreciate the bigger picture. He was thinking of Margaret. After all her years of effort so that John could become a priest, he shouldn't give up now. John Bosco should also consider his responsibility to look after his mother. As a secular priest he could have a good parish, be a good parish priest and would have the means to look after his mother, so she could spend the last years of her life without financial worries. This seemed to Don Dassano, to be the way forward and in accordance with God's command. A friar's habit and a vow of obedience which might send him anywhere, seemed to him to be an unfair way to treat a mother.

He said to John, *Before giving you the documents you need, I want to talk to your mother.* As soon as he could, he went up to the farm at Sussambrino, and sitting there with a glass of wine, as was the custom, he spoke quite openly to Margaret, *John has asked me for documents to support his entry into the Franciscans. They would willingly accept him and he could finish his studies for nothing. Let's be clear, I am not against the idea, even if John seems to me to be better suited to working in a parish because he relates well to people. But I want to make it clear. Margaret, you are not wealthy, and you are getting on in years. As a parish priest, your son could help when you can no longer work. However, if your son is a friar, he will be lost to you. For your own good, I am convinced you should dissuade him from this decision.*

Mamma Margaret respectfully listened to the words of the parish priest, but as she listened she became very upset. Did the parish priest think that she had helped John to become a priest so he could look after her in her old age? She had never given this a moment's thought! The more she thought about it the more upset she felt. The following morning, Margaret wrapped herself up well in her shawl. She told her family she was going to see John. She set off, rosary in hand, to walk the fifteen kilometres to Chieri.

Half a page written more than one hundred years ago

The Salesian, Don Lemoyne wrote the Life of Mamma Margaret. When Don Bosco reviewed a draft copy in 1886 he remarked *this is half a page where I do not even want to alter a comma:*

> She greeted her son with a smile. *The parish priest, out of kindness, has told me that you wish to become a religious. Is that true?*
> *Yes, mother. I didn't think you would mind.*
> *All I am concerned about is that you think seriously what you are about, and that you then follow your vocation without worrying about anyone else. The*

most important thing is the health of your soul, your salvation. The parish priest wanted me to dissuade you from your decision, in view of the need I would have of your help in the future. Let me be clear about this. I do not come into it, because God comes before everything. Don't worry about me. I want nothing from you; I expect nothing from you. Never forget this. I was born in poverty. I have lived in poverty. I want to die in poverty. In fact, I'm telling you now: If you decide to become a secular priest, and by some misfortune become wealthy, I will never come to visit you, I will never put a foot in your house. Never forget it.

Don Giulio Barberis, one of the first Salesians, who made sworn deposition for Don Bosco's process of beatification, testified:

Mamma Margaret said these words with such an air of authority, that at times Don Bosco told me that even when he was seventy he still felt moved whenever he recalled his mother's words.

At that time one of John's best friends, Emmanuel Savio noticed how upset and undecided he was. When John told him why, he said to him, *Why not ask Don Cafasso's advice? He is the best priest ever born in Castelnuovo. He is only 23 years old, but in Turin he is already the spiritual director of many important people.*

John followed his advice. Don Cafasso listened to the anguished explanation of his dilemma. Finally, and very calmly, he said to him, *Finish your last year of public schooling. Then enter the seminary. Divine Providence will let you know what is wanted of you. As far as finance is concerned, don't worry, someone will provide.*

From that day onwards Don Cafasso became John Bosco's spiritual director, supporting and encouraging him. He would remain so for the rest of his life. For him, *Someone will provide* were not just mere words. Don Cafasso, who was the confessor of many wealthy Christian folk, would always find money for him in times of need, money that was strictly necessary.

Don Lemoyne concludes this part of the story with the following words, *Once his mother knew that John had made up his mind, she was happy too, 'as long as you do God's will'.*

20. Son in the Seminary

John finished the final year of school, *Rhetoric*, in 1834-35. During the summer, before entering the seminary, he went for his holidays to Sussambrino, to join his mother and his brother's family.

It was when farmers were at their busiest. The wheat had to be cut, threshed in the hot sun, separated from chaff, sifting the grains on huge sieves, benefiting from any little puff of wind. Then it was time to harvest the corn, and to stack the long bundles so they would dry in the sun. For the children, summer was a great time. They would run amongst the harvesters bringing them bottles of fresh water, giving a hand to push the empty trolleys that would be filled with sheaves and ears of corn, gathering up the ties which would bind the sheaves.

John, as soon as he had finished his last exam, set out on the dusty white road from Chieri to Buttigliera and then crossed to where the fields were. Sussambrino welcomed him with the crowing of roosters and the happy clamour of relatives. The wheat stood golden between the vineyards, where the grapes were already reddening. John grabbed a sickle and joined the row of reapers.

Mother of a Seminarian

After the work of the harvest, while the shadows lengthened, there was a brief pause in the life of the Monferrato farmers, a *catching of breath*. In this pause between summer and autumn, Mamma Margaret helped John, who on August 16th would be twenty, to get himself ready for the seminary. She was about to become the *mother of a seminarian.*

Material items were needed: a trunk, the clerical cassock, a good mattress, (straw mattresses were not allowed in the seminary). As soon as they found out in Castelnuovo that Margaret's son was entering the seminary, there was almost a competition to help him. Don Bosco would say, *I always needed people right from the earliest years. When I had to don the clerical habit, since my mother had no means, there were those who provided it, someone the biretta, someone else the collar, and yet another the cope.* It was October 25th 1835.

Grand words

October 30th 1835 was the last day John Bosco would spend out of the seminary. He went to see about conscription and was declared fit enough for military service. However, since he had been accepted into the major seminary, by law he was declared *a cleric*. Summoned by Archbishop Chiaverroti, he put on the long black cassock which went from collar to heel.[21] It was a way of telling everyone, *From now on I will be a priest, and I will behave as a priest.*

In his memoirs, Don Bosco recalls that day:

October 30th of that year, 1835, I was to enter the seminary. The small trunk was ready. My relatives were all happy: I more than they. It was only my mother who was pensive. Her eyes followed me round as if she wanted to say something to me. On the evening before my departure she called me to her and spoke to me these unforgettable words, *John, you have put on the priestly habit. I feel all the happiness any mother could feel in her son's good fortune. Do remember this, however; it's not the habit which honours your state, but the practice of virtue. If you should ever begin to doubt your vocation, then for heaven's sake, do not dishonour this habit. Put it aside immediately. I would much rather have a poor farmer for a son than a priest who neglects his duties. When you came into the world, I consecrated you to the Blessed Virgin. When you commenced your studies I recommended to you devotion to this Mother of ours. Now I say to you, be completely hers. Love those of your companions who have devotion to Mary. If you become a priest always preach and promote devotion to Mary.*

My mother was deeply moved as she finished these words, and I cried, *Mother, I thank you for what you have said and done for me. These words of yours will not be in vain. I will treasure them all my life.*[22]

In these words we see the great faith of a peasant mother. Faced with her son going to the seminary, like a farmer faced with a field full of ripened wheat she forgets all the work, the difficulties, the sufferings that have gone with it up till now. Her son is about to achieve the first goal of the dream he had at nine years of age, she only feels *consolation*, only sees the *good fortune* of her son. This faith has been supported by a total trust in Mary, to whom she consecrated John as a newborn child, and entrusted him as he took his first steps to school. Her faith was real, not something illusory. In the short span of her life she had also seen priests who had dishonoured their habit, their mission. So she put her son on guard against this with the strong words, *Better not a priest than a bad priest.*

---

[21] For this reason it is called *talare*, in Italian, which means *heel*

[22] Memoirs of the Oratory p 126

Seminary Life

From autumn 1835 to the summer of 1841 John Bosco lived in the major seminary in Chieri, in that vast edifice, once a convent of the Filippini sisters and adapted for the seminary in 1828 by Archbishop Chiaverroti. For eight months a year the seminarians led an almost monastic lifestyle. The daily timetable was exact and covered every minute. Everything was listed on a sheet, hung in some corner, near the bell tower. Hours, half hours, quarter hours, all strung together. At the end of each hour the bell ringer would come up to the bell rope and pull it. At the sound, the entire community would go out, come in, speak, fall silent, study, pray. The first thing they were taught was that the bell was the voice of God.

The wake-up bell rang at 5 am. Cold water was ready in the large jugs. Then the line of seminarians would wind down to the Church for the daily Mass at 7 am. Breakfast would follow, then school, dinner, recreation, school again, study, supper. At 9 pm, evening prayer, then immediately after, time for bed. At five o'clock next morning, before dawn it would start all over again, from the beginning, for eight months on end. Dinner and supper were in silence, during which they listened to a reading from the Bible in Latin and then some Church History. The cuisine was very simple. *We eat to live, not live to eat* was written on a card in the refectory.

Although Mamma Margaret was not part of this rigid monastic existence, her influence, instead, continued discreetly. The evening before he left she had said: *Do not dishonour the habit.* And John noted from the very first months that there were individuals already in the seminary dishonouring the habit they wore. He writes:

> I have to say that in the seminary there were many clerics of outstanding virtue, but there were also others who were dangerous. Not a few young people, careless of their vocation, go to the seminary lacking either the spirit, or the will of the good seminarian. Indeed, I remember some companions indulging in very bad language. Once, a search amongst a student's personal belongings unearthed obscene books of every kind. They were expelled when their true character came to light. But, as long as they stayed in the seminary, they were a plague to good and bad alike.[23]

Mamma Margaret had also told him, *Love those of your companions who are devoted to Mary.* And Don Bosco writes:

> As for my companions, I stuck to my beloved mother's advice. That is, I fraternised only with companions who had a devotion to Mary and who loved study and piety. I chose some who were well known as models of virtue. They

---

[23] Memoirs of the Oratory p 132

were William Garigliano, John Giacomelli of Avigliana and Louis Comollo. These three friends were a treasure.

The seminary fees were a hundred lire per year. This was a heavy sum for Mamma Margaret. At the end of the first year, because of his good marks, John gained a reduction to sixty lire. For the rest, Divine Providence came to the rescue, silently directed by Don Cafasso.

21. Guiding Her Son

The feast of Saint John the Baptist is June 24th. For the seminarian John Bosco it was the beginning of the long school holidays: four months. This was the time when Mamma Margaret could have John all to herself. During the six years of ecclesiastical studies, November 1835 - June 1841 she had him around for a total of twenty months. John felt that, after the long lectures from the professors, sometimes very dry, he could return to his mother's quiet but very lively tutelage. Up to 1839 John spent those summer months at Sussambrino. In 1840, he went back to The Becchi, where Anthony had built a small house, and Joseph was finishing off building his, both in front of the old cottage of their childhood.

Children had arrived and the two families were at peace with one another. Anthony and Anna, in 1840, already had four children: eight-year-old Francis, Margaret at six, Teresa at three, and John still in the cradle. Joseph and Mary had two children, five-year-old Philomena and two-year-old Rosa Domenica. Philomena, with her wonderfully shy smile, was John's favourite. He was her godfather and saw her grow up like a pretty flower in Sussambrino. Mamma Margaret was the happy grandmother of them all.

In those summer months Mamma Margaret, through her silent example, guided John towards a new and basic attitude to spirituality. At the time, and for many years afterwards, the young cleric-seminarian lived in recollection with his books and the sacred sciences. He had to be with the parish priest and the church almost constantly.

John Bosco had just arrived back in Sussambrino, and joined with Joseph and his mother in the full swing of summer work. It was natural enough for him to take off his black cassock and join them in the reaping, as he himself recalls, cutting the hay, picking grapes and then preparing for the vintage. Happy with the harvest, the Boscos and the Febbraros would joke from one furrow to another, sing at the top of their voice, kneel down together and pray the Angelus when the bells in Castelnuovo and Buttigliera would join forces across the valley at noon. What a joy it was to sit on the grass, passing the bread, the salami, and wine to each other after taking a large swig. It was a noisy, real happiness, blessed by the Lord.

A New Kind of Spirituality

Mamma Margaret, watching the behaviour of her future priest, never said to John: *It would be better for you to stay away from this. These are not the sorts of things priests do.* Instead in the late evening, before they would lay down exhausted on the sack of corn leaves, better than the seminarian's mattress, she would remind him: *Now let's say the Rosary all together, and not forget our evening prayers.*

John Bosco starts to move towards and grow in a new style of spirituality, here amid the vineyards of Sussambrino, under his mother's gaze. In those times a certain suspicion was attached to the attitudes typical of the poor; noisy cheerfulness, singing, talking loudly, running, joking, laughing out loud. These were things seminarians disapproved of and which the seminary forbade as *vulgar.*

John Bosco, thinking about it, saw that seminary regulations were right, but also wrong. The attitudes of the poor, which he encountered, which his mother experienced as a deeply Christian and human individual, were neither vulgar nor pernicious. Many of these attitudes, in fact, contained values that were strictly gospel values, and simple folk were the bearers of these values, often forgotten by those who feel superior: simplicity, the love for simple things; solidarity, standing together; consideration for the little ones, the unimportant ones; the capacity to discover happiness in small things, understanding, speaking, listening, explaining to one another; considering sacrifice as a normal price to pay in life; humble prayer; love for and confidence in Our Lady; cheerfulness even if it is noisy; seeking the greatest comfort in friendship; readiness to share one's bread with the poor; the hope for a more just world as something to bring about with God's help, but also through the work of our hands and the sweat of our brow.

These were the Gospel values, which John Bosco, on reflection, discovered in his mother's life, and also in his own, because they were values he had absorbed from her. These would be the behaviours forming his spirituality, the popular spirituality he would hand on to his Salesians. He would have the ecclesiastical world discover that this is a true, authentic spirituality able to bring one to the *holiness of the altar.* He would see, and have others see, that as well as a holiness of ecstasy and visions like that of Maddalena de` Pazzi, there was also the holiness of the young student struggling away with his Latin grammar like Dominic Savio. If there are saints who contemplated God by writing masterpieces of theology like St Thomas, there are illiterate mothers like Mamma Margaret who served God heroically amid pots and casseroles, socks to mend and children to teach and blow their noses for them.

This *popular holiness* of which John Bosco will be *Father and Teacher* in the Church, at first would cause perplexity, then would be recognised and spread through the countryside, the outskirts and poor suburbs, among the humble children of God. Francis de Sales pulled holiness out of the convents and planted it in the homes of the laity. John Bosco pulled holiness out of cultured environments and planted it among the crowds of ordinary people.

Philomena is Enchanted

When the first rains of autumn came, and the seminary was still a long way off, because school only recommenced on November 3rd, John took up the carpenter's plane, operated the bellows again at the forge, fixed the hoes and the ploughs, and hammered away on the scythes worn down by summer labours. Four-year-old little Philomena was enchanted by the way her Uncle John used the plane on the wood, making so many white curls with it, making the fire in the forge shine red and bright and causing a shower of bright sparks with the hammer. She would sit near him where he had called her, while he made beautiful little dolls for her.

In the early freshness of the morning, some young students would also come along, and John would cheerfully help them with their Latin. Amongst them were John Bertagna, (who later became Bishop of Turin and would testify in the process for the beatification of Don Bosco), George Moglia, the child he had seen while looking after the cows on the farm, and other boys. John taught them with loving-kindness. The handful of lire the families gave him for his services were used to buy his books for the following school year.

Under the Parish Priest's Gaze

On Sundays, when farming work had ceased, John Bosco went up to Castelnuovo, and under the gaze of the parish priest, Don Cinzano, set up a *kind of oratory*. After Mass and in the afternoon he had recreation with the boys. They weren't vigorous games, because they were coming from a week of hard work and needed to rest a little:

> I would tell them stories, and teach some hymns. Seeing that some of them were sixteen or seventeen years old but deprived of the truths of the faith, I was keen to teach them daily prayers and other important things. Around fifty youngsters would attend, they loved me and obeyed me as if I were their father.[24]

Don Cinzano looked on, and scratching his head, thought, *And he wanted to go to a monastery!*

---

[24] Memoirs of the Oratory p 140

Mother's Medicine

In the seminary at Chieri, John Bosco completed the first two years of philosophical studies called, respectively, *logic* and *physics* (1835-37). In 1837 he commenced the five years of theological studies. By a concession from the Archbishop, John reduced these to four, but took all the examinations.

In the spring of 1839, after a winter of intense study and the loss of his friend, Louis Comollo, John was afflicted by a serious kind of depressive exhaustion. The classic symptoms of this were: loss of sleep and appetite, notable loss of weight, melancholy and a tendency to remain isolated. The depression, as always, was long and exhausting.

The doctor did what he could with the medicine of that time. Instead of sending him back to the quiet surroundings of the family to work on the farm for a while, he ordered him to bed for a month. The cure was so inappropriate that John got much worse. Not knowing what else to do, the doctor declared him *gravely ill*, which in the language of the day meant *in danger of death*.

Mamma Margaret, when told her son was in bed for some days and was not improving, came looking for him with a large loaf of meal bread baked in the family oven and a bottle of well-matured wine. The gesture made by this fifty-year-old peasant woman is a moving one. She was told her son had been sick for some time, and she knew that the illness which affected many farmers at the end of the season was malnutrition, when the sacks of flour were almost empty and there wasn't enough to eat until the next harvest. There was only one treatment for this: eat well, chew on good bread and drink good wine. In those hills they didn't know much about illnesses with complicated names.

John had very little appetite but did not want to disappoint his mother. After she had gone he took a piece of the bread, washed it down with a mouthful of the wine. He kept eating. Sip after sip, mouthful after mouthful, the wine was drunk and the bread was eaten. John drifted into a heavy sleep *lasting that night and two days to follow.* When he awoke he suddenly felt much better.

22. Mother of a Priest

On Saturday June 5th 1841, John Bosco was ordained priest by the Archbishop of Turin, Louis Fransoni. The ordination took place in the Archdiocesan chapel dedicated to Our Lady Immaculate. During the retreat in preparation for this great day, he wrote a verse from a psalm in a small exercise book: *Who will climb the mountain of the Lord? The one with clean hands and pure heart.* Looking back on his life, he could see that his hands, from the time Mamma Margaret had first joined them in prayer, had remained clean. He had never done harm to anyone. His heart, beating along with his mother's, had remained pure.

I celebrated my first Mass, he writes in simple terms *in the church of St Francis of Assisi, assisted by my illustrious benefactor and director, Don Joseph Cafasso.* Don Bosco wanted to say his second Mass at the altar in the Consolata, the great Marian shrine in Turin. Lifting his gaze, he saw in the small, precious painting up there, the woman shining like the sun, who had said to him in the dream seventeen years before, *Make yourself humble, strong and energetic.* He almost could not believe it, but his mother had believed, and had laboured and suffered to that day so that the dream could come true. Now the time was beginning when *he would understand everything.*

The Bells of Castelnuovo

The Thursday following was the feast of Corpus Christi, a Holy Day of Obligation. Don Bosco said his First Mass for his own town. The bells pealed at length. The people had gathered in the great parish church to see Margaret's son who had become a priest. The evening of that day, when they were alone, Mamma Margaret said to him, *You are a priest, you say Mass, and from here on you will be close to Jesus. Remember, however, that to begin to say Mass, means to begin to suffer. You will not notice immediately, but little by little you will see that your mother has told the truth. I am sure you will pray for me every day, whether I am alive still, or dead. That's enough for me. From here on, think only of the salvation of souls and have no thought for me.*[25]

Ascanio Savio of Castelnuovo, for the beatification of Don Bosco said under oath:
I saw the parish priest Don Cinzano greet Mamma Margaret, warmly and say to her: *You are a generous and holy mother. The Lord has preserved you so that you can kiss the consecrated hand of your son John.*

---

[25] Lemoyne Life, p 114

The Joys of the Grandmother

In the five months that followed, while Don Bosco gave a hand to the parish priest and lived in the presbytery, Mamma Margaret went back into the shade of her normal peasant existence.

At the end of October 1841, advised by Don Cafasso, Don Bosco went up to Turin. He entered the *Convitto Ecclesiastico,* a post-graduate seminary, directed by Don Guala and Don Cafasso. The latter had told him, *Come and learn how to be a priest.* For three years, 1841-44, Don Bosco stayed at the Convitto, and little by little started up his Oratory. In the two years following, 1844-46, Don Bosco wandered through the northern outskirts of the city, looking for a stable location for his boys and his Oratory. Only by Easter of 1846 would Don Bosco find that stable location for his Oratory in the Valdocco area, a brief walk from the River Dora.

All that time Mamma Margaret remained at The Becchi, in Joseph's new house, working as a peasant farmer and being a grandmother.

23. Margaret Prays with the Boys

In a very short time Don Bosco had noticed that the situation for young boys around Turin was a disastrous one, even if few others seemed to notice. Only a year before, the renowned liberal, Lorenzo Valerio,[26] had written:

> Whoever has set foot in a factory and especially in a silk factory will have been sadly shocked seeing that swarm of youngsters with an unwitting curse constantly on their lips, emaciated, cut and sweaty, covered in dirt, pushing each other around, and living by petty theft, fraud, heading for big crime; and would be horrified of the sad future awaiting those little blond heads, needing really very little to ensure that they had all the habits, graces and virtues of childhood.

These were the boys John had seen in his dream at nine years of age, whom Our Lady had entrusted to him, and for whom he and his mother had sacrificed so much for seventeen years.

When Don Bosco came to Turin, 6170 adults and 1115 children worked in the silk trade and were being paid just 50 cents a day. The children were forced into this work by their families, because children were strong enough to look after a machine, they worked thirteen and sometimes fourteen hours a day, with the managers ready to whip out a stick if they fell asleep. The floor was bare earth, the temperature hot because *it was needed to properly spin the cotton and silk*. If the boys' lungs were weak, they began to spit blood. In the spinning mills they stood there with blank looks on their faces and died like flies.

The little bricklayers endured similar conditions, attracted as they were to the building works springing up around the outskirts, the young chimney-sweeps, boys in search of any kind of work in the iron works, in carpentry shops and ordnance factories. They came in flocks, like migratory birds, from the valleys of Piedmont and the Savoy, and from the plains of Lower Lombardy.

Workshops and Factories

Rendu, Bishop of Annecy where the great cotton factory of the Savoy-Piedmontese State was, wrote a memo to King Charles Albert in 1845, describing the inhuman conditions of the workers, especially child labourers. He demanded *a law to bring justice to the factories*. But at the same time the *Congresso degli Scienziati Italiani*,[27]

---

[26] Igiene e moralità degli operai of seteri (Hygiene and morality in the silk works)

[27] Italian Congress of Scientists

which brought together the richest capitalists in the Kingdom, replied that *child labour in workshops and factories is absolutely necessary to keep up with foreign competition.* Those who spat out blood and their lives to give Piedmont the funds for subsequent wars of independence were buried in huge anonymous, common trenches. The average life span of a worker, when Don Bosco came to Turin, was 17–19 years.

The richer people believed in something that left Don Bosco angry and amazed. They believed that the horrendous situation in which so many families were living, forcing them to send their children to work in the factories, the widespread theft and delinquency amongst young people who refused to die of hunger, was not created by any lack of humanity or injustice on the part of the owners. No one believed that the schedules, the salaries, the state-protected health conditions imposed, were the cause of the constant poverty of working families, the theft and delinquency of many youngsters *trying to survive.* The real causes, according to the richer classes, were malice and the sheer laziness of the poor.

The Causes of Poverty

In the years around 1840 there were Catholics in Turin who dedicated their lives to helping the poor, but given that they belonged to the better off and even noble element in society, their style was rather paternalistic. They behaved in a superior way seeing the poor as lesser beings, in a lower league. Behind the charity of those days some of the better-off were of the opinion that the poor were poor because they were bad, abject poverty was the result of sin. Don Bosco, who had lived in a poor Christian family, totally disagreed with this view.

He went out to meet boys in search of work, through Turin's streets, boys who had lost their jobs because they were unable to work, boys who stole shopping bags at the Porta Palazzo market, because they were hungry. He also met them in the prisons, where they were thrown together, big and small, to become a *school of organised crime.*

No sooner had he succeeded in making friends out of them, than he set to, offering them his entire strength and imagination. On Sundays, and whenever he was free, he taught them to read, write and add up, and he took it upon himself to check their wages to see that their employers were not cheating them. He also had them praying, singing and playing, so they could rediscover their youth and their faith. He looked for humane employers, who would give them work without exploiting them. Was this not what Our Lady had asked him to do in the dream when he was just nine years old?

For all his faith and youthful strength, Don Bosco was only human, and in 1842 Mamma Margaret saw him return, from time to time, to The Becchi, tired and exhausted. He told her he was bringing the boys together at an Oratory, and that he had so much to do. When he came back to The Becchi in October 1845, he was more exhausted than ever. It took a month of good food and complete rest to revive him.

Bad News Comes to The Becchi

In July 1846 Don Bosco did not come to see his mother. Instead, she received news that he was gravely ill, possibly at death's door. Joseph and Mamma Margaret left that day for Turin. They found Don Bosco in a room that the Marchioness di Barolo had made available to priests working in her charitable works, not far from the general market at Porta Palazzo.

Margaret saw that her John was whiter than the sheets covering him. *He had a serious lung inflammation and was coughing up blood.* The Marchioness di Barolo had sent for her doctor, who came to attend him several times a day. The symptoms were the same as she had seen when she sat at the bedside of her dying husband, Francis. Pneumonia had taken the father of her children when he was but thirty-four years old. Now she feared it might also carry off John, her son.

Margaret told Joseph, *You go home to your children. I will remain here. I will send you any news.* She took out her rosary and large handkerchief from her skirt. With her right hand she wiped the perspiration and the blood from John and fingered the rosary with her left hand, saying every now and again: *Holy Mother, I consecrated him to you. Don't let him die.*

Praying Together

She soon found she was not alone in her prayer. The poor frightened boys from the Oratory, whom she had never met but who had unbounded love for Don Bosco, had found out about his illness. The message had gone round the poor of Turin, *Don Bosco is seriously ill. Don Bosco is dying!* That evening, Mamma Margaret saw groups of poor boys arriving. They still wore their dirty work clothes. She saw them crying, praying with the words of the poor: *Lord, don't let him die. If he dies, who will look after us?*

Mamma Margaret suddenly understood the great good her son was doing with his Oratory, which had only gained a stable location in the Valdocco area a few months previously. As night fell, more boys crowded in through the door:

Signora, just let me see him.
I just want to tell him something very important.
If Don Bosco knew I was here, he would let me in.

John Baptist Francesia, was one of those frightened boys, who later became a great Salesian priest. He recalls that Don Bosco heard them, and asked his mother to open the doors and let them come in. He said, *I might die. But let nobody have any doubt: if I die, the Lord will send others to take my place.* Mamma Margaret watched the boys crowd round her son's bed. The smallest stood on tip-toe and said: *Don Bosco, it's me!* She also saw boys praying to Our Lady with the kind faith that works miracles. Once they knew she was Don Bosco's mother, some said, *We are going now, because we want to spend the night praying at the Consolata.*[28] These were boys who had worked all day and were already totally exhausted.

Our Lady heard the prayers of Don Bosco's boys and his own mother. He wrote in his memoirs:
> It was a Saturday evening, I thought it was the last night of my life: That's what the doctors said, who came to see me. I was feeling devoid of all strength because of the constant loss of blood. In the late evening I felt myself drifting off to sleep. When I woke up I was out of danger. Doctor Botta and Don Cafasso, when they came to see me in the morning, said they went to thank Our Lady at the Consolata for the grace received.

Mamma Margaret witnessed how overjoyed the boys were. Batistin Francesia wrote:
> That morning, more flowers than you can possibly imagine were bought, and strewn along the way from the house of the Marchioness di Barolo to the Oratory. The flower-sellers, at the market at Porta Palazzo, amazed that so many youngsters had come to buy flowers, were asking what feast day it was, what saint.
> *They are for Don Bosco,* the boys said, *the one who comes from the Oratory. He was deadly ill and now he's recovered.*
> *Who is Don Bosco?*
> *He is that priest who looks after us boys and teaches us so well.*
> *Has he been ill?*
> *Very much so; but come to the Oratory today and we will have a great feast.*[29]

---

[28] The nearby shrine of Our Lady

[29] Short popular Life

Don Bosco Recovers

As soon as he was able to, leaning on a stick, Don Bosco went to the Oratory. They went with him singing and crying. Mamma Margaret also went with him and she, too, was crying. They sang a hymn of thanksgiving to God, and surrounded Don Bosco with enthusiastic acclamation. Francesia wrote:

> The older ones got him to sit down on a stool, and they carried him like a king on a throne, while the youngest ones shouted all around him and threw their flowers at him. They filled the Oratory chapel. The Blessed Sacrament was not as yet kept in that very poor little chapel, but the small statue of Our Lady was there, she who had given them back their Don Bosco.

John Bonetti, another of Don Bosco's boys, recalls his words:

> God has given back my life for you. I will spend all of it for you. This I promise to do until the Lord calls me from this earth. And you will help me!

The doctor prescribed a long convalescence and absolute rest. And as soon as he heard this, Don Bosco took his mother's arm and together they set off towards the hills. He promised his boys, who would be looked after by that great priest Don Borel, *When the leaves begin to fall, I will return.*

24. A Mother's Sacrifice

There were nine grandchildren there to welcome home their uncle, the priest, and their grandmother to The Becchi. Four were Joseph's: Philomena, Rosa, Francis, Louis born that year and still in his mother's arms. Five were Anthony's: Francis, Margaret, Teresa, John, and Francesca. Mamma Margaret kissed them all, hugged them all, and then cast an affectionate and smiling eye on the chickens, who had also run to meet them. This was her home, where she returned to live like a queen. In the evening, when she saw them all around saying the Rosary, she felt so much at home.

Don Bosco too, truly felt so much better. The shy smiles from the nephews and nieces, the open friendship of his brothers, his mother's quiet affection and her good cooking, gradually gave him back his health and his strength.

His mother said to him towards the end of August, *Now that the sun has lost its strength, it's time for you to give some thought to putting everything you are doing in Turin back into order. I don't want you coming back to me every year torn to shreds.*

Don Bosco strolled amongst the vines where the grapes were darkening already amongst the green and golden leaves. He thought of Valdocco, calmly planning the future. In November, on his return, he would go and live in the two rooms he had rented at the Pinardi house, above his Oratory courtyard. He would take up the work which he had only just begun. The evening classes for poor boys would have developed by now. This was so that the boys would not need to spend all their lives in the spinning-mills and on building-sites. He would provide accommodation to most of the poorest ones who had nowhere to go at night and risked prison by spending the night under the porticos. Then, if God helped him, he would take some of the boys from the factories, and set up some workshops in the Oratory itself.

Margaret Saves John from Gossip

In the Pinardi house, where he was going to live, there were some other lodgers. How come a priest was going to stay alone among that lot? Besides, not far away, Madame Bellezza ran a somewhat dubious hostelry called, *La Giardiniera*. Drunkards would sing away until early morning. Any priest living alone in that area would find himself a prey to gossip. This problem worried him.

Going for a walk to Castelnuovo he went to speak to the parish priest, Don Cinzano. He explained the situation and asked his advice. The priest didn't need to think about it for long. He said: *You have your mother. Get her to come with you to Turin. You will have an angel at your side.*

Don Bosco stood there stunned for a moment. *But she is 58 and she has never been to the city. Here she has her sons and grandchildren who adore her, and she is so happy here. At Valdocco she would be swapping poverty for misery. It would be too much of a sacrifice for her.*

Don Cinzano knew Mamma Margaret well, and he immediately retorted:
> Sacrifice? And what do you think your mother has been doing all her life? She has already worked great miracles of sacrifice, privation, patience and humiliation so you could become a priest.[30]

I Am Ready to Go

Don Bosco waited until October. Then he plucked up courage and said:
> Mamma, you have seen how much the boys of the Oratory like me, and how poor they are. At the beginning of November I am going back to them. Once you said to me that if I became wealthy you would never enter my house. You have seen how poor I am, and how my poor boys have so much need of help. Besides, living alone in that area is risky for a priest. Would you come and be a mother to my poor boys?

In his memoirs, Don Bosco describes what happened next in just a few words, *she understood what I meant and replied straight away: If you think such a move is God's will, I am ready to go right now.*[31]

I think these words alone are sufficient to prove that she is a saint. They contain heroic faith, rock solid. They were not said by a young person, in the prime of life, but by a lady of fifty-eight years, which at that time was considered *old*, for life and work had taken its toll. *If it pleases the Lord – I am ready – immediately.* These are the identical words with which Our Lady accepted God's invitation.

She was not the mother of a priest about to head off to stay in her son's quiet and respected presbytery. Margaret accepted that she would be going to live in two rooms on the squalid northern outskirts of Turin. She had seen them when she went down to see her son at death's door. She was going to act as mother to those poor youngsters who were praying with her like angels that her son would not die,

---

[30] Sworn testimony of Ascanio Savio. Positio p 212

[31] Memoirs of the Oratory. p 296

their clothes worn and their faces filthy with smoke and grime. She would not be the mother of a parish priest; her job would be sewing clothes, showing boys how to wash their faces, sharing her soup with them.

These words were no mere rhetoric. One of those young lads, Michael Rua, who spent ten years with her and spoke with her in confidence as he did to his own mother, said under oath that *she knew the serious inconveniences she would encounter. But, as she said, if it pleased the Lord, I am ready to go straight away.*

God Calls Her to Leave Home

Don Bosco writes in his memoirs:

> My mother made a great sacrifice; because at home in the family, although not well off, she was in charge of everything, everyone loved her, and to young and old she was a queen. We sent ahead some of the more necessary items. These were delivered to our new lodgings. My mother filled a hamper with linen and other things we would need; I took my breviary all four volumes, the missal, some other books and copy books. This was our entire fortune (all we possessed). We set out on foot.

They set out on foot on November 3rd, after All Saints and All Souls day. Margaret had lived more than half a century on a small patch of land. Each autumn she had watched flocks of birds in the sky, migrating southwards. Now God's will was also asking her to migrate to the outskirts of a city she had barely glimpsed before. She was migrating with her son along that mysterious path traced out in a childhood dream, which she and he believed then and still believed.

Turin, with its population of 120,000 inhabitants, greeted them from a distance with its bells. They went down towards the Dora, crossed it, passed along the narrow streets of the Borgo Dora populated with *migrants and brigands*, and arrived at the two rooms prepared as best he could for them by Don Borel.

As Rollini, one of the artists dear to Don Bosco, has faithfully depicted her, Mamma Margaret in a long peasant woman's dress, black with white dots, her coloured shawl, and her favourite headscarf which she wore on feast days. The headscarf was a sign of modesty (and at the time a way of keeping dust out of long hair), that all married women wore them and had done for centuries. It was a kind of *chador* that combined modesty with a degree of elegance. Everyone accepted it. Women began not to wear it around 1946, when American fashions began to come in.

Don Bosco wrote:

> Arriving in those almost empty rooms, my mother said, jokingly, *At home I had so many things to worry about, I'll be much more at ease here, nothing to look after, no one to command.* Together, mother and son began to sing a song popular at that time, *Woe to the world if it should learn we're just penniless strangers!*

A boy, Stephen Castagno, heard them, and news quickly spread as it does amongst the poor, *Don Bosco is back! He's brought his mother!* The 3rd November 1846 was considered by many older Salesians as the true beginning of Don Bosco's work.

Michael Rua, the small boy who grew up with Mamma Margaret and became the first successor of Don Bosco in the Salesian Congregation, asked all the sons of Don Bosco to celebrate the fiftieth anniversary of this occasion. In the letter he sent to Salesians in Italy, France, Spain and South America, he wrote, *November 3rd 1846, this is a wonderful day, the beginning of all Salesian Works.*

Boys in a Circle

November 8th was a Sunday and was celebrated as a feast day. Don Bosco and his mother, seated in the middle of the Oratory yard and surrounded by a circle of a hundred boys, listened to the songs and greetings prepared for them. Mamma Margaret enjoyed the songs, but more than everything else she was so pleased to see the joy on the face of her son. It seemed that Don Bosco's return had enkindled hope in the boys, the hope of leading a good and honest life in a city that had treated them so harshly.

25. Starting Again

Raimondo, Chicken Thief

Don Bosco was in a hurry to get going again. For this reason in those first weeks his doctors, Don Cafasso and even the Archbishop were concerned. *I was told not to hear confessions and not to preach for two years. I disobeyed.*[32] Don Bosco knew that the young people from the poor parts of the city needed God, but that God at this moment relied very much on him, and also on his mother to save them.

Two months before their return a twelve-year-old boy, Raimondo, had been arrested by the police. In the boys' Reformatory *The Generala,*[33] the specialist and educationalist, Charles Fissiaux, stared at the boy and wrote in his report:

> His legs, emaciated by poverty and vice, are tied in chains.[34] His hair is infected with lice. His frail body is covered in filthy rags. From his appearance, his numbed moral and physical faculties, we can judge the devastation wrought in this small human body by debased habits, irresponsible pleasures and criminal pursuits.

What would these debased habits, irresponsible pleasures and criminal pursuits be? The *criminal pursuits* of this twelve-year-old, which horrified the abbot-teacher Charles Fissiaux? We can read folder 53 file 87, headed: *Raimondo R, outline of particulars*. The historian, R Audisio, has researched and written it up. The following has been drawn from his research:

> The boy had been arrested and put in chains because he had been found with a box of four dead chickens and could not say where they had come from. His particulars are, twelve years of age, illiterate, unemployed. His mother is dead and his father is an itinerant scrap-metal dealer. He was first arrested when he was eight-years-old, caught while sleeping under the porticos of the Piazza del Palazzo Civico. He was told to go back to his family. Two months later he was condemned *as lazy, a vagrant suspected of theft of wine on the Piazza Carlina*. He paid for these *mistakes* with a year of confinement in the Saluzzo prison, where those detained were not kept separately but together, regardless of age and crime committed. He lived, then, for a year with hardened criminals, and this was the only schooling he had received in life.

---

[32] Memoirs of the Oratory p 293

[33] Opened on April 12th 1845

[34] They used chains rather than handcuffs

Since coming out of Saluzzo prison he was arrested six times in two years, always *for theft* or for *sleeping under the porticos*. Eating and sleeping were the *debased habits, the blameworthy pleasures* that Raimondo R. and other poor kids like him were unable to avoid. Misappropriating *four dead chickens, stealing a few mouthfuls of wine from the huge barrels in Piazza Carlina* were *the criminal pursuits* reported by Abbot Fissiaux. He was also arrested as a *fugitive from home, a vagrant and beggar who associated with unruly types.* The police, who were there to protect the peaceful existence of the middle classes could not understand that Raimondo had no *home* to return to, because his mother was dead and his father an itinerant. So he went round as a beggar because he did not want to die of TB and hunger, as happened to some of his companions and he tried to sleep under the porticos along the Via Po coughing, and covering himself with sheets of newspaper.

The Abbot Fissiaux's educational method

This time, for *four dead chickens* they sent him to the *Generala* instead of prison, the reformatory opened the year before to *reform those unhappy youngsters who, either because of their parents´ bad example or led by bad companions, or by unbridled attraction to misdeeds, began their errant life early, in idleness or worse.*

At the *Generala,* Raimondo would have been put to work like a young cadet in a tough military training camp. He would be awakened at 5 am and his day marked by discipline, and silence for most of the time. The colonel who wrote up the schedule would have in mind *young delinquents to be straightened out through rigorous military discipline.*

The daily rhythm was so inhumane that in the first months they had to forcibly put down the young inmates' revolts. On December 16th 1845 a tumultuous uprising broke out: five prisoners hurled themselves at Brother Sereno, one of the assistants charged with looking after discipline, and tried to stab him to death. In the turmoil they cut off a finger. Only then did the guards manage to immobilise them. No one thought to mitigate the rigour of their lives. Instead the disciplinary regime was tightened. They were punished with higher fences to make sure they didn't escape.

The educational result was written up in a few words on July 11th 1846:
> Given their freedom after a year of *re-education* according to the Fissiaux method, these juveniles would become involved in much worse delinquency than before: for every carpenter[35] doing well for himself, fourteen boys abscond as soon as they cross the threshold of the Generala.[36]

---

[35] Minusiere

[36] Audisio *119*

Abbot Fissiaux was considered at the time *the greatest of educators*. Comparing his methods with those of his contemporary, Don Bosco, one begins to understand the educational revolution the priest from The Becchi, with his mother, brought quietly to Turin and then to the world. More than once Don Bosco would say: *My system of education? Not even I know what it is. I bring up the boys as my mother brought us up.*

The immigration wave in the 1840s

From the year 1840, Turin saw a growing wave of immigrants, especially youths, poor and abandoned, in search of any means of survival. The lowering of infant mortality brought about by smallpox vaccination, made obligatory by Napoleon, resulted in an excess of labour in the countryside, construction of new homes in the city, growth in the production of silk, wool, cotton, tobacco; which caused poverty and unemployment in the countryside.

The miserable wages, one lira a day for men, sixty cents for women, fifty cents for children, did not allow any savings, and obliged everyone in the family to go on a frantic search for work to survive. One lira enabled a worker or bricklayer to feed himself, if he was prepared to do another thirteen hours of work the following day. Sixty cents were enough to buy two kilos of poor quality bread, while well-to-do women would spend the same at a café for a sorbet or two hot chocolates.

Young immigrants, just arrived, put themselves on the labour market as bricklayers, manufacturing workers, clerks, shoemaker's assistants, or assistants to barbers, carpenters and butchers. Thirty seven per cent of immigrants, in the 1840s, settled in the outlying Borgo Po and Borgo Dora, on the borders of which was the Valdocco area. In ten years these two suburbs saw their population quadruple.

In the damp Borgo Dora, lung diseases, some of them fatal, were common. In this suburb, according to police records, in the 1840s young thieves and boys without family multiplied in number. They went in for vagrancy and begging. Older youths and younger boys often banded together in gangs involved in theft, pick-pocketing and mugging.

Mamma Margaret's Second Family

Right there, in the Valdocco area, it is hard to say whether by choice or by providence, Don Bosco came to live with Mamma Margaret. The priest from The Becchi had a simple but decisive plan, drawn up during the days of his forced rest. In the first place he would re-open and enlarge the evening school, convinced that poverty was especially the result of ignorance. Then he would begin to accommodate, by day and by night, boys without a family. The regulations and the timetable were not drawn up by a colonel in a military establishment but by his mother who appreciated family life, and would make those boys her second family.

26. Abandoned Boys

In November 1846, Don Bosco recommenced evening classes for his little friends. On December 1st, since the number of pupils had grown out of all proportion, he rented the entire Pinardi house for 710 lire a year. He called on all his priest friends from the Convitto days for help, Don Chiaves, Don Musso, Don Carpano, Don Pacchiotti and others.

He set up school in the rooms, the kitchen, the sacristy, the choir and other parts of the church. Don Bosco recalls:

> In the winter of 1846-47 our schools got excellent results. In middle school we had 300 pupils each evening. As well as science, our classes were enlivened with plainchant.[37]

In late evening, when school was over, Don Bosco was worried. Many of the youngsters had no family, and had no idea where they would sleep. They would end up in squalid public dormitories, or, if they did not even have the few cents needed to stay in those dank rooms, they slept under bridges or porticos where they risked arrest for one of the usual three crimes: vagrancy, thuggery or running away from home.

Problems in the Barn

Along with his mother, he set up a kind of barn to take some of them in. But it did not go well. He writes, *Some of them repeatedly made off with the sheets, others the blankets; and in the end even the straw was stolen and sold.* This happened many times. There was enough to be discouraged about, but faced with the constant poverty of so many boys, Don Bosco and his mother did not let themselves become discouraged.

In from the Rain

One very wet evening in May; when it had rained all day in Turin and it was as cold as a winter's day, Don Bosco and his mother had lit the fire in the hearth. They had just finished their meagre supper when they were disturbed by an insistent knocking on the door. Don Bosco went to the door to find a young boy there. Tall and thin, drenched to the skin, he shivered from the cold. *Please, please can I come in for a moment? I just can't go any further.*

---

[37] Gregorian chant was used then in the Church's liturgy

Later, Don Bosco recalled the event:

> My mother acted immediately. She took him into the kitchen, sat him down in front of the fire, and while he was warming himself and drying off his clothes, she gave him some bread and soup. I asked him if he went to school, if he had any relatives, what sort of work he had. He mumbled a reply, *I'm an orphan; I've come from the Valle di Sesia to find work. I only had three lire, but I've already spent that and I can't find any work, so I'm starving.* Bursting into tears he cried, *I've got nothing and I'm worth nothing.*
>
> I asked him if he had made his First Communion. He answered, sorrowfully, *No.* He soon finished the food my mother had given him, he certainly had been hungry. I asked him, *Where are you going now?* He looked totally lost and replied, *I've no idea. Could I stay the night here*? With that he burst into tears again and my mother cried with him. I wasn't sure what to do. Some weeks before, we had let some boys sleep in the hayloft because they had nowhere to go. They had stolen the blankets and the mattresses. My mother said to him, *If I knew you weren't a thief, I would help you, but I've already been robbed, and how do I know you won't steal from us?* The boy, still shivering from the rain, looked at her very seriously, *Lady, I know I'm poor, but I've never stolen anything.*
>
> My mother turned to me, *If you want I'll look after him tonight, and tomorrow God will provide.* I replied, *As you wish.* My mother went with the boy to look for a few bricks. She made four little piles with them, laid some planks across them, and put a mattress on top. The first bed in the Oratory was made. My good mother then gave him a little talk about the need to work, about being honest and about religion. Finally she invited him to recite his prayers. *I don't know any,* he answered. *You can say them with us,* she said. Then, so that everything would be safe, she locked the kitchen. This was the first boy to stay.[38]

We do not know the precise day of this event, but in the calendar of the poor, it was very significant. That rainy evening saw the beginning of Mamma Margaret's second experience as a mother. The first was at The Becchi, where she had given life to two sons, Joseph and John. The second began that evening, on the outskirts of Turin, and lasted nine years; the last nine years of Mamma Margaret's life. She gave life and hope to more than a hundred orphaned, poor and abandoned boys.

---

[38] Memoirs of the Oratory p 314

Down from the Tree

The second boy to be taken in was Felice Reviglio. He told his own adventure story when he testified for Don Bosco's beatification. He was fourteen-years-old, and got into the Oratory by climbing a wall while the others were at church. He met Don Bosco, was won over by his kindness then made his confession to him. Though at first he did not even know the Hail Mary, he became a good Christian. He began to attend evening classes. But things were not going well at home.

The boy's mother was a poor woman; she drank, blasphemed and blamed priests for all the woes in the world. She discovered, by chance, that her son was going to Don Bosco's Oratory. She lost her temper, she had been drinking, and threatened Felice that she would beat him if he went near that priest again. He answered her, *If I learned at the Oratory to steal, fight and be bad, then you would be right to stop me. But there they teach me to love my mother and father, to do my duty; they even teach me to read, write and add up. I want to go and I want to keep going there.* Her answer was a blow across the ear, then she looked around for an axe she kept in the house.

In fright, Felice ran out the house, towards the Oratory, with his mother in pursuit. He was more agile than she was, so he arrived at the gate first. He hoped it would be open, since the boys were about to arrive for evening school. Instead it was closed, because Don Bosco was out. He knocked and cried out in desperation. Mamma Margaret, who by chance was near the window, heard the knocking. Looking out, she saw the boy climbing a large mulberry tree which grew close to the gate. Felice had climbed the tree, and was hiding from his mother. Although it was the beginning of autumn, the tree still had plenty of leaves.

As Mamma Margaret went out, Don Bosco arrived. *My mother was convinced I had gone to the Oratory,* Felice said later. *A long discussion took place between her and Don Bosco. Listening unobserved, I was only afraid that someone would look up at the tree and discover me there. It was providence, for sure, that nobody saw me. Neither Don Bosco nor my friends, who meantime had arrived for evening school had seen me, and could reassure my mother that I couldn't possibly be there.*

Certain she was being fooled, the woman threatened, *Alright then, I'm going to the police, and I'll see that the priests pay every cent they have.* Don Bosco replied, *I'm going to the police too. I have a few things to tell them about your behaviour, my good woman, and this seems to be just the right time to do so.* The mother muttered a few more threats and disappeared.

Mamma Margaret, who had seen Felice climbing the mulberry tree, pointed the boy out to Don Bosco. They quietly called him down. He did not answer. Fearing some accident, Don Bosco climbed the tree. Felice, seemed to be having a nightmare, he started to yell, and became very agitated. It would not have taken much for the two of them to fall out of the tree. Gradually the boy calmed down and began to cry. Don Bosco persuaded him to come down and gave him to Mamma Margaret, while he went off to teach. His mother prepared something hot for supper, and then said to him, *Tonight you sleep here. It would not be prudent to go home*. She set up a bed for him for the night.

The following day, once the effects of the wine had worn off, the boy's mother regretted her behaviour. Felice tells the story:

> The following day, I met my mother who had come back to look for me, and I got her permission to stay at the Oratory. That was when I became the second boy taken in by Don Bosco. Gradually our numbers grew. I was given soup and bread each day, and could pick the vegetables growing in the garden outside to supplement this. I knew Don Bosco's mother, with whom I lived for a period of ten years, and I can say in all truthfulness that she was a woman of outstanding piety, simplicity, prayer and sacrifice. I found out from her that, after she became a widow at twenty-nine or thereabouts, she had many proposals of marriage, but refused them so she could attend to her children's education; something that cost her so much.

In 1847, along with the Valsesia boy and Felice, another five boys were accepted as *boarders*.

Mamma Margaret's Jewellery

With the first boys now living in, expenses increased. Don Bosco, even though he hated doing it (and he said this many times), began knocking on the doors of the nobility and the better-off citizens. Sometimes he was given an offering for his boys, while at other times all he got were insults. His first benefactress, nevertheless, was no countess, but his mother. He writes:

> My mother sent for her wedding trousseau, which up till then she had jealously preserved intact. From some of her dresses we made chasubles. My mother also had a little gold necklace and some rings. They were quickly sold.[39]

John Bonetti became a boy at the Oratory in 1855, he spent one entire year with Mamma Margaret. He wrote:

---

[39] Memoirs of the Oratory p 297

Regarding the good woman's detachment from worldly things, even though she had sold off those precious items, she recalled that it caused her some pain. Once I heard her say: *When I saw those things in my hands for the last time, I felt a certain regret and turmoil. But as soon as I realised this I said to myself, Go on, you couldn't have better luck than this: feeding and clothing poor children, and doing honour to the Heavenly Bride in Church. I felt so happy after doing it. If I had another hundred trousseaux I would have still got rid of them all without any regret.*

Turin's other face

The year 1847 ended, shrouded in the Dora mists. The end of the world would seem to break out in the year that was just beginning: Revolution in six European capitals, King Charles Albert's Constitution granted, the first war of independence against Austria. According to the history books the *wonderful story of the Risorgimento* began: Turin becomes *a city crowded with soldiers going off to redeem Italy, the streets filled with people clapping and tossing flowers.*

It is a false image. The Turin where Mamma Margaret, Don Bosco and his poor boys lived was a very different city. Those who described *Risorgimento Turin*[40] had never set foot in the working class suburbs: Vanchiglia, Borgo Dora, Moschino, a network of streets around the Palazzo di Città, the City Hall. The politicians only went for their walks through the first blocks along Via Po. They stopped in the café Florio and San Carlo, to discuss politics over a glass of vermouth costing a worker's daily wage. They never entered the wretched taverns frequented by the poor and miserable, like *La Giardiniera* where drunken shouting often interrupted Mamma Margaret's sleep. The romantic description of *Turin, capital of the Risorgimento* makes one forget Turin's other face: overcrowded, hungry, aggressive, and miserable.

Mamma Margaret was a heroic citizen of this other Turin. She never walked around the elegant monumental palaces in the city centre. She lived as one of the nameless Turinese, and looked after large numbers of the poorest citizens. She belonged to those, for whom the 1817 famine was more important than the movements of 1831 and where making ends meet counted for much more than the concessions granted by the Constitution. For this reason history books never show an interest in people like her, outlining battles instead of describing scenes of daily life, the woes within the population, the orphans fed daily by an illiterate widow and her son, the priest.

---

[40] I take my words from historian Umberto Levra

27. The Year of Revolutions

1848 was the year of Revolutions. They began in Paris on February 24th, destroying the monarchy of Louis Philippe. They continued like a game of dominoes, Vienna - Berlin - March - Budapest - Venice and Milan.

Overwhelmed by events, on March 4th in Turin, Charles Albert granted the Constitution[41] and on the night between the 23rd and 24th March, declared war on Austria. 60,000 men left for the front led by the King and the Crown Prince Victor Emmanuel. All horses, needed for pulling artillery and carriages, were requisitioned in the city. The city, without the usual rumble of carriages, suddenly went very quiet. Notwithstanding these events, which arrived like a summer storm, life for the *ant's nest* of people, eking out a desperate living in the suburbs, carried on as usual. They waited patiently for things to pass as they struggled to afford dinner and supper. In 1848 there were many Piedmontese and Turinese, like other Italians, completely indifferent, if not hostile, to the National Risorgimento.[42] Mamma Margaret and Don Bosco, in the Oratory, were amongst those who simply found the war to be a source of problems.

The first boys from the Oratory were called up. Batistin Francesia, who lived through those days recalls:

> When the 1848 war was declared, many of those young men who were amongst the first to attend the Oratory, had to go to war. Don Bosco, like an affectionate father, gathered them together, gave them useful advice, telling them to be sure he would pray for them. They wrote back to him often, and vowed to return quickly to Turin, to their beloved Oratory. Don Bosco followed them on a map, marking the battle locations, placing some pins here, some there and then told us about our distant friends. The thought of danger and the affection that bound us together made us pray that the Lord would bring them back quickly. The boys, especially those almost adults, went to Holy Communion almost every Sunday for their soldier friends. With how much affection we waited for news! If Don Bosco announced that he had received some letters, there was immediate silence as everyone gathered around to listen. Sometimes we cried at hearing what they had to go through and at other times rejoiced. When we heard of the defeat in Novara in 1849, we were all very sad.

---

[41] A Constitution not written by delegates of the people but granted by the King

[42] Umberto Levra

Mamma Margaret too, prayed for those boys, and their mothers. She had come to know some of them while she prayed for her own dying son. Already older lads, workers, arrived from distant parts and found in Don Bosco their only help to become honest citizens and good Christians. And now, though they had been forgotten in their own time of need, they had been called to war, to shoot, to kill and to order others to kill.

Mamma Margaret had never needed a church to pray in. The churches were always a long way from her home. But now she had a little chapel nearby, the one used by the Oratory boys. There was no tabernacle yet with the Blessed Sacrament, it was difficult to get permission from the Bishop. But there had been a small statue of Our Lady there for some months, to the right of the altar. It was a poor, papier-mâché statue costing 27 lire. Mamma Margaret, when she was tired, went into the chapel, sat on the last bench and said her Rosary, looking at the statue of Our Lady. She understood them, she was their *Madonna*. They were both mothers, they knew how difficult it was to bring up children, how painful it was to see them suffer, how difficult it was at times to understand them, and to remain quiet when you didn't understand them.

Ascanio, the first leader at the Oratory

In February the seminary was closed. The clerics were invited to return to their families. One of them, Ascanio Savio from Castelnuovo, asked the Archbishop if he could continue his studies at the Oratory. Don Bosco had known him for five years, and knew he would be an excellent leader for his boys, so he supported the request. Ascanio became the first *cleric-assistant* at the oratory. He recounts his experience there as follows:

> I knew Don Bosco's mother when I went to the Oratory; she was called *Mamma Margaret* by all of us, by strangers, even by the bishops themselves. In our village they held her in the highest esteem. My parish priest said she was a holy woman, and that she had performed miracles to help her son become a priest. I saw that this woman was always revered by the young people at the Oratory, as if she were their mother, and really, she showed herself to be a mother to everyone.

A frenzy directed against priests

The Constitution had granted freedom of the press. It had taken public education away from the Jesuits, as well as the right to censure books. What came to be called *intellectual dictatorship* was directed not only against the Jesuits, but also against all priests. Don Bosco writes:

A kind of frenzy seized the minds even of youngsters, who would get together at various points in the city, in the streets and squares, believing it was praiseworthy to insult priests or religion. I was attacked many times at home and in the streets. One day as I was teaching catechism, a gun shot came through the window, passing through my cassock between my arm and my ribs, and making a large hole in the wall. Don Borel also escaped miraculously from a pistol shot. It was a perversion of thought and ideas and I could no longer trust people as domestics; so all the housework was done by my mother and myself.

For Mamma Margaret these were times when she feared for the life of Don Bosco. There were difficult moments. Someone advised Don Bosco to temporarily close the Oratory, and wait for better times.

Straw mattresses in Church

Don Bosco instead came up with a brilliant idea. He thought of a five day retreat to bind them closer and produce vocations. It was a reckless kind of enterprise: like planting saplings in a hailstorm. Mamma Margaret was going to be overburdened by extra work; and would employers give a five-day *holiday*, so their workers could say prayers and listen to sermons?

Don Bosco went ahead. He spoke to and gained the agreement of around fifty boys, from among those already living-in and those who came for evening school. Then he started out on the pilgrimage around the workplaces. He explained that the retreat would make the young workers better, more obedient. Many of the employers just shut the door in his face. Around twenty of them instead, who knew Don Bosco, accepted after lengthy hesitation. At this point, Don Bosco asked permission of the families, those who had families, or next of kin. Finally he spoke with Mamma Margaret. He told her, half in jest, half seriously, that he had decided to take up the role as cook by her side for a week, and would be inviting around twenty boys to dinner and supper. His mother, who already was a confidante of all the boys, laughingly asked him if he had decided to take on the dishwashing role too.

The more difficult problem to resolve was finding twenty places to sleep. Don Bosco, in fact, wanted the retreat to be enclosed, so it would be more effective, that is without any external contacts day or night. Joseph Buzzetti, the boarder in whom Don Bosco had the most confidence, and to whom he had already given most of the administrative tasks to do with Mamma Margaret, remembered with a smile how much effort he went through with Mamma Margaret to find places for those twenty straw-mattresses. They tried everywhere, under the stairs and in closets. In the end they decided to put them all in the chapel, between one bench and another. *They won't be very comfortable but if they are tired they will sleep.* Then they had to do the impossible: find plates and cutlery for everyone, keep everyone's plates full for dinner and supper, for five full days.

Each day of the retreat consisted of Mass celebrated in the morning, and four talks, two in the morning and two in the afternoon. The topics were life and death, judgment and God's mercy, heaven and hell. The centrepiece of the retreat was a good confession made, according to Don Bosco, *as if it were the last one of my life.* Some priests came in from outside for confessions, but almost all the boys went to Don Bosco. The effects of the retreats were wonderful. Don Bosco, on the almost illegible page 144 of the manuscript of his memoirs writes:

> It went very well. Many boys for whom I had laboured in vain for a long time really gave themselves to virtuous living. Several entered religious life, others while continuing in the secular life, became models in their regular attendance at the Oratory.

In the left-hand margin of the same page, Don Bosco wrote, in small print, eight names and surnames of those first boys, adding, *they always remained good Christians.*

All this meant extra work, for Mamma Margaret, Joseph Buzzetti and especially for Don Bosco, but the spiritual benefits were so special that Don Bosco, despite the cost and sacrifice, repeated it each year. The chain of retreats which started with twenty Oratory boys, went on uninterrupted until Don Bosco's death, and was always a source of good vocations for Christian and religious life.

28. The Battle for Mamma Margaret's Garden

During the spring of 1847, when the first boy was taken in, Mamma Margaret, like a good housewife, turned part of the yard into a garden. She worked there for a while each day, because though turning ground into a garden seems easy, in fact, it is heavy and skilful work. Cultivating, manuring, planting and watering began to produce lettuces, capsicums, tomatoes, onions, beans, carrots and garlic. In a letter of Don Bosco to a countess, amongst other things there is a request to have a handful of broad beans which his mother has asked for to plant in the garden. Don Bosco helped his mother put up a small hedge around the garden, so that nobody would trample on it during lively recreations. Mamma Margaret's garden, for the ever-increasing number of boys living there day and night, was a real treasure.

The Era of the Gangs

The northern boundaries of Turin, at the time, were dominated by the *Cocche*, gangs defined in police reports as *groups of dissolute youths living in the streets surrounding the city, a danger to peaceful citizens*. The departure of soldiers for the war resulted in gangs like those belonging to *Gambero*, the most notorious, *Moschino*, *Ballone*, *Santa Barbara*. They attacked people, throwing stones and using sticks, and robbed them. There were pitched battles between them for control of funds and territory. These were real battles in the fields, with dead and injured such as Paolo, sixteen years of age, who died on April 11th from knife wounds and was left lying in the fields near Borgo Dora.

Don Bosco recalls with sadness, *Those battles never ended*. Sometimes he went to call the police, but he could not always find people willing to put themselves in the middle to separate the combatants. Sometimes he would do it himself, using strong-arm tactics, and would receive the occasional boot in the face. That was when Mamma Margaret had to bathe his face in cold water, and chide him for having rather too much courage, *Can't you see that even the police won't tackle this situation? One day you'll get a knife in the back and that'll be the end of all your dreams!*

War Games

Instead of following his mother's words, Don Bosco thought a little and came out with some odd words which Mamma Margaret herself couldn't quite understand, *So the boys want a war*? He said, *Well, I'll let them have one, but in the Oratory yard*. Joseph Brosio, a young friend of his had been a Bersagliere, a sharp-shooter, and knew something about battles. Don Bosco invited him to put on his uniform and plumed helmet, to bring his trumpet and come to the Oratory to organise *military exercises*. Brosio accepted but said, *What about the guns? Where are the guns? We can't have exercises and play war games without guns*. Don Bosco had friends in the Government. He asked the War Ministry for about a hundred obsolete weapons with the barrels replaced by wood for his boys to play with. They agreed, and one Sunday afternoon the *great war games* began.

Batistin Francesia, then just a young boy recalls:
> It was beyond description, when, after dinner, the rooms were opened, all the equipment was there ready for recreation. There was a rush to grab a weapon, minus its barrel with a big piece of wood there instead. What military exercises then took place! What an atmosphere!

And with what trepidation, we can imagine, Mamma Margaret set herself up near the garden, stick in hand to defend it from any soldier!

The war games continued for a long time, on sunny Sundays from 1848 to 1850. People came running as soon as they heard the blast of trumpets and the shouts of the combatants. Marches, retreats and mock bayonet charges. Then the two battalions, on the order of the *Bersagliere*, would form up on opposite sides of the courtyard; at the battle signal they would all shout *Hurray!* then aim their guns for the charge. Then it was time for bayonet charges, the fight would begin, and they would head for the flanks to catch the other side by surprise. In the end it would take all the commander's and Don Bosco's authority to separate winners and losers and declare the battle over. People would clap and Don Bosco would run amongst the combatants with a bag full of sweets.

Mamma Margaret's Crisis

It was probably one Sunday afternoon in 1850 that disaster occurred. The number of boys, Don Bosco and Mamma Margaret had taken in, was around twenty-five. It was hard work to look after them all, keep them clean and keep their clothes presentable. Mamma Margaret would hang out their shirts to dry between the rows of beans, even on Sundays. In the afternoon on that particular Sunday the great battle began.

John Bonetti, one of the boys who spent two years with Mamma Margaret and enjoyed her company, and appreciated her motherly affection describes the disaster as follows:
> On one occasion the small army did something which really displeased someone whom, after Don Bosco himself, they loved most dearly. I mean, Mamma Margaret. Her small garden, carefully seeded and looked after with

great attention, provided lettuce, garlic, onions and a vast range of herbs, including mint and sage. The *Bersagliere*, having called the mob together and divided them up into two, set out to entertain the spectators with a mock battle. He distributed the weapons, and fixed which of the two groups had to finally concede defeat in battle. He was especially careful to remind the victors that once they reached the hedge around the garden, it was time to retreat. Having given the command, the battle flag was raised, the two groups shouted out *Hurray*, and with one group on one side of the courtyard and the other on the opposite side they began battle moves, aiming their wooden rifles. Hearing the solemn shout, the well-ordered charges and counter-charges, the slow advance and retreat, you could have sworn you were in a real battle. Bystanders loved it, and clapped, and shouted *Great, Bravo*. The applause spurred on the warlike spirits of the combatants. At a certain point the winning side, overrunning their opposition, forgot their orders, and the battle spilled over into Mamma Margaret's garden. The hedge was ruined; plants fell, everything was trampled on and ruined. The *Bersagliere* shouted, sounding the trumpet, but in the noise of the laughter and clapping of the spectators nothing was heard. When the two sides came back into order, little remained of the garden. At the sight of it all Mamma Margaret, perhaps believing that the assault had all been planned to make the battle something really spectacular, was very upset when she turned to her son, and said: *Look, just take a look, John, what they have done to me. They have completely destroyed the garden.* Don Bosco reassured her saying, *Mother, what can you do about it? They are young*. To the general, then, mortified about what had happened, he offered some kind words of encouragement.[43]

It was that evening, probably, that Margaret felt the entire weight of her sixty years. The boys had gone off to sleep, and she, as usual, had a pile of clothes in front of her to mend. Together with Don Bosco, she was mending shirts and shoes which the boys had left at the foot of their beds. She had to have them ready for the morning, because they had nothing else to wear. At a certain point Margaret put the needle down next to the oil lamp. *John*, she whispered, *I am tired. Let me return to The Becchi. I work from dawn to dusk, I am a poor old lady, and those rascals are always ruining everything. I just can't carry on any longer.*

Don Bosco looked at his mother's face and felt a lump in his throat. He couldn't find the words to reply to her. There wasn't anything, which could console the poor woman. He just made a gesture: He pointed to the Crucifix hanging on the wall and

---

[43] Cinque Lustri, 310 ff

his elderly mother understood. *Everything you have done to one of these little ones, you have done to me,* the Lord had said.

She lowered her head back to the torn trousers, ripped shirts, and continued mending. She never again asked to return home to her grandchildren. She would spend the rest of her years amongst those noisy, uncouth boys who needed a mother. Just that she would sometimes need to lift her eyes to the Crucifix to ask for strength.

29. The Death of Anthony

The year 1849 began with very sad news: On January 18th, at The Becchi, Anthony died. He was only 41. In recent times, when he came to Turin to market, he would pass by Valdocco to find his mother and brother. He told his mother about the children who were growing up. Anthony spoke of the taxes the Government was imposing on everyone, stealing the bread from their mouths to pay for the war.

On that cold January day, Don Bosco and his mother were on their way up to The Becchi to attend the funeral and console the widow and the children. Mamma Margaret was thinking of that son who was so sad. In seeing first his mother, then his father die, then the grandmother who was his last link with his family, he had built up an ocean of sadness in his heart and mind. Margaret had been twice as careful with him as she had been towards Joseph and John, but it seemed to be of no account. Angry more at life than at her, sometimes he would shout out *Stepmother*, making her suffer deeply. At times, overcome by jealousy towards his two brothers whose mother was alive, he would savagely beat them, and she would have to forcibly remove them from him. He would not forgive anyone for the least offence. Yet she behaved with kind yet firm love towards him too. She recalled one evening in particular. After a very upsetting day, while they were saying their prayers, she stopped Anthony from saying the *Our Father* with the others. They had come to the words *Forgive us our sins as we forgive those who sin against us*. Calmly but firmly she told him, *It would be better if you didn't say these words. They would be a lie. You never forgive anyone. How can you ask the Lord to forgive you if you are always seeking revenge?* For Margaret, at the time, it seemed that, as a mother, she had failed Anthony. Yet as the years went by, her sincere love bore fruit. He became a good father to his family, very strict but affectionate towards the children.

Bankrupt and Broken

On March 23rd 1849, in Piedmont, everything collapsed. The war against Austria was lost in the bloody battle of Novara. Charles Albert abdicated the same day, and the crown went to his son, Victor Emmanuel II, who signed the armistice on March 26th.

Austria exacted 200 million lire from Piedmont as war reparation. (This was an enormous figure that meant the State was declared bankrupt, and all money in circulation lost its value). Genoa declared itself 'independent' from Piedmont, a *republic*, and the first act of the new King was to retake the city by assault.

Even though, a few months later, Austria reduced the war reparation to 75 million lire, the Government had to double taxes, increase excise, and impose extraordinary duty. Everyone experienced terrible poverty.

Simple Food

The Oratory too had to tighten its belt. Bread was the staple diet. The cheap bread eaten by the poor cost 37 cents a kilo, and the boys would consume on average half a kilo each. But as well as bread they needed hot food. When the young workers and students, who lived in, came back at midday, they went straight to Mamma Margaret's kitchen. They would hold out their mess-tin for food, and ask: *What is there today, Mamma?* The large pot was boiling on the fire, and Mamma Margaret would answer *Rice and potatoes* or *pasta and broad beans* and less frequently, *polenta and chestnuts.* This last announcement would be welcomed with enthusiasm. Dried chestnuts, white and sweet, boiled with polenta, made a sweet porridge, which everyone liked.

Everyone had a spoon in his pocket, which he would wash afterwards along with his tin. Anyone could go out into Mamma's garden and help themselves to lettuce, tomatoes or capsicums, and make a nice salad. Every now and again there was a slice of meat. Never cheese and fruit. The pump was the bar, and served fresh water.

Mamma Margaret's chickens would wander around amongst the boys eating. Mamma Margaret loved the chickens, they provided eggs to give some substance to the soup, and they, for their part, were on the lookout for some crumbs.

Mamma Margaret's Sister

In 1850, all of a sudden Marianna, Mamma Margaret's sister, came to give a hand. Don Lacqua, the parish priest of Capriglio, had died, and she had been his housekeeper since 1824. She was sixty five, and she was not about to recommence the life of a farmer. She had asked her sister and her nephew Don Bosco if she could come to give a hand, and she was welcomed with open arms. The boys were also fond of her, and called her *Magna*, which in Piedmontese means *Aunt*.

In the large paddocks surrounding the Oratory, the city laundries hung out long lines of washing. Now that the numbers of boarders at the Oratory were growing so fast and now that she had her sister's help, Mamma Margaret was able to *rethink* the laundry. She set up a washhouse. Every fortnight was time for a change of linen. *Up to that moment*, Don Bosco recalls, *there were boys who never changed their shirts; they were so filthy that no employer would take them to work in his workshop.*

But if there were nasties nesting in their washing, there were also lice to be found in their hair. Only in 1860, to put an end to this plague, had the Ministry of Public Education decreed that students' hair be cut short. In Mamma Margaret's day they wore their hair long, sometimes combed but often unkempt and unwashed. Mamma Margaret, and also Don Bosco and Joseph Gastini who had acted as barbers, when they saw a long head of hair, gave a hand with the scissors. Young Battista Conte recalls that one day, during the haircut, he complained to her: *You're cutting it all in steps and stairs, Mamma!* She said, *Don't worry, these stairs will take you to heaven.*

A Mother to All

In 1850 the friendship between Mamma Margaret and young Michael Rua began, a boy without a father and poor in health, who would become the right arm and successor of Don Bosco. He offers a precious and lengthy sworn testimony:

> I came to know Don Bosco in the September of 1845. I was eight years old. Brought there by a friend, I began to attend the Oratory and for some years I went there occasionally. Following that, towards 1849, I began to attend regularly. In 1850, advised by Don Bosco, I began the study of Latin to become a priest. When I entered the Oratory, as a boarder, I had 36 companions who were there already. From then on I lived with Mamma Margaret. I came to know that truly Christian and pious woman, generous and courageous of heart, yet always prudent. She dedicated herself to educating her children well, then those of her adopted family. I and all my companions always admired the goodness of her heart and her generous charity. She had left her home to come and subject herself to the effort and serious task of looking after so many poor orphans. We all called her Mamma out of the respect and filial affection we felt for her.

From the time he was a baby Don Bosco had been nourished on the milk of love and the fear of God. Until he was 11 or 12 years old he was exclusively taught by his mother. She made sure he always attended the parish functions on feast days.

He gave everything he had for his poor orphans, including his mother's jewels and wedding dress. She was in agreement with this.

When he had no other companion beside his mother, a dish prepared on Sunday had to last till Thursday evening, and on Friday, another small dish that lasted Friday and Saturday.

With regard to what I have said, I have based it on what I have known personally and on reports from Don Bosco's mother.

30. To Dream of a Church

In winter, in the Oratory chapel the snow and rain came in, and the floor was covered in mud. When it was full of boys, summer and winter, you could smell the heavy atmosphere and the odour of cheap clothes. It was the same smell you would find in any working-class home at that time; but when Don Bosco invited a priest to hear confessions with him, he saw him recoil from the stench of humanity.

The chapel had become too small. The ever-growing crowd of youngsters coming to the Oratory every Sunday, even with the windows open, made it hard to follow Mass or hear the words. Don Bosco did not want just to be in charge of a yard where they played war games; he wanted to be an educator and a priest.

One February evening in 1851, Mamma Margaret was mending the clothes while the boys slept. Next to her, Don Bosco was mending two shoes. At a certain point, mouth half full of nails, Don Bosco murmured: *I want to build a church dedicated to St. Francis de Sales*. Mamma Margaret's needle fell out of her hand. *A church! But we can't even feed these poor children with soup and bread! Haven't you noticed that in Turin there is more poverty than there is air? Who will give you the money to build it?*
If you had the money would you give it to me?
Of course I would give it to you. But we don't have any money!
God and Our Lady are more generous than you, don't you want them to give us the money?

As she did on other occasions, Mamma Margaret tossed her head, thinking *How am I supposed to argue with a son like this?* But she had to admit that when he came up with crazy ideas, he always seemed to succeed with them. He had succeeded with the boarders (despite the theft of blankets and mattresses), with the retreats (despite the protests of the clergy), with the war in the courtyard (and that seemed impossible). She kept on sewing and praying, telling Our Lady from one bead to the other: *You have suffered, Who can understand children?*

The plan for the new church was drawn up by Cavalier Blancher, and immediately after, the impresario, Federico Bocca came along. He organised the digging of the trenches.

Mamma Margaret saw the money come from her son's new idea: he got the authorities to assign the proceeds of the *citizens' lottery* which the Mayor organised once a year for a *worthy cause*. Don Bosco and his friends made great efforts to bring in the lottery prizes. In all there were 3,300, offered by merchants and industrialists in the city, but preceded by four excellent gifts, offered by the Pope, the King, the Queen Mother and the Queen Consort. The gifts were put on display in Via Dora Grossa, and created a real hubbub around Don Bosco's lottery. This helped to sell a mountain of tickets. The lottery was drawn in the City Hall, the Mayoral offices, on July 12th 1852, and the winning numbers published in the *Giornale Officiale.*[44]

Work on the Church proceeded well, and Mamma Margaret saw that the boys themselves, in their free time, gave a willing hand to the bricklayers.

A Small Boy from Castelnuovo

In the first days of November 1851, Don Bosco, returning from a visit to the parish priest of Castelnuovo, brought with him a boy of thirteen, who had lost his father. He was called John Cagliero, and he would be, together with young Michael Rua, one of the boys most attached to Don Bosco. He would become the first Bishop and the first Cardinal of the Salesian Congregation, which Don Bosco was about to found.

John Cagliero, speaking under oath for Don Bosco's beatification, recalled his first days at the Oratory:

I always remember with pleasure the moment I entered, on the evening of November 2nd. The house was in its beginnings. Don Bosco introduced me to good Mamma Margaret saying, *Here, Mamma, a young boy from Castelnuovo who wants to become good and to study.* The good mother replied, *Oh yes, that's all you do, go looking for boys to help, while you realise we have no room.* Don Bosco, smiling, added, *Oh! You'll find some little place for him. This young lad, as you can see, is not very big, and we can get him to sleep in the breadbasket; and then hang him up on a string, and there, we've found a good spot for him, just like a canary cage.* His mother laughed, and meanwhile went off to find me a place.

The following morning I saw that everything in the cottage was very poor. Don Bosco's room was low and narrow; our dormitories on the ground floor were narrow with some paving stones from the street for a floor. No furnishings except our mattresses, sheets and blankets. The kitchen was miserable and devoid of stoves, except for some tin ladles each with a spoon. Knives, forks and napkins came many years later, bought or given by some pious and charitable person. Our refectory was a shed, and where Don Bosco ate, a small room close to the well, which served the school and the place for recreation. All this kept us in the same lowly conditions we had been born in and where we found ourselves taught by Don Bosco's example. He enjoyed

---

[44] Official Journal

it when he could serve us in the refectory, help us keep the dormitory in order, clean and mend our clothes and similar services.

I personally came to know his mother, Margaret Occhiena from Capriglio. She became our good mother for five years, while she was alive. The virtues of good Mamma Margaret, as we called her, were those of a truly Christian mother, kind, agreeable, patient and extremely charitable towards us poor orphans. She was a simple country woman. She was a model for Christian mothers.

The Powder Works Disaster

In the spring of 1852 the roof was almost ready on the new church when disaster struck. On April 26th, towards noon, a terrible explosion was heard, and a dense plume of smoke covered much of Borgo Dora. All of Turin was suddenly affected. A second stronger and more violent explosion occurred, and fear was everywhere: the Turin powder works, located in the lower part of Borgo Dora, had blown up with a tremendous explosion. The explosions wrecked all the homes in the Borgo and the windows in half the city. There were 28 victims. The Oratory roofs were damaged. The new church, still without doors and windows and with part of the roof still to be covered, was hit by the shockwave, but suffered minimal damage.

Mamma Margaret and all the boarders received a terrible fright. Don Bosco, with the older boys, ran to where the disaster had occurred to see if there was need for volunteers and to carry the injured to hospital. It was up to Mamma Margaret, with the boys who had stayed behind, to pull off the broken tiles from the roof, select the most habitable spots left, and take the beds there along with other things needed. When Don Bosco returned, they all thanked the Lord that nobody had been hurt.

The Cottolengo hospital where thousands of incurable people were cared for, had some rooms destroyed and many inmates with cuts and abrasions, some serious. Dozens of the patients were injured. Others wandered around the ruins, confused.

Don Bosco had already succeeded in paying 35,000 lire for the new church. He needed another 30,000. This final amount, obtained from the lottery, he put aside. When however he saw the tremendous damage sustained by the Cottolengo, he divided the 30,000 lire in half, sending half to the Superior of the Cottolengo. He wanted this to remain a secret, he had only taken advice from Mamma Margaret. However the Archbishop was told of it, and he wrote a beautiful letter, calling the Cottolengo and the Oratory, *two works close to each other, visibly demonstrating the Lord's hand.*

Mamma Margaret had told John many times about the history of Saint Martin, the soldier who had given half of his military cloak away to a poor man shivering from the cold, who then in a dream saw the Lord who said, *Martin covered me with his cloak.*[45] Now she saw her son going halves with the poor from the Cottolengo, not his cloak, but half of the money he needed to finish the church. Her story had borne good fruit. And providence would give him what he needed.

---

[45] The story of Saint Martin was depicted in many of the Monferrato Churches

31. Mamma Margaret's Proverbs

John Baptist Francesia was a young boy from San Giorgio Canavese in Turin. Poverty had brought them to the city. At eleven years of age the young boy was put to work in a foundry, with a wage of thirty-three cents a day. He was working amongst adult workers who frightened him with their blaspheming and shouting. On the feast of All Saints in 1850 he was invited by a friend to go to the Oratory. He recalled his first impressions:

> That excitement of young people, that urge to have fun, all that light-heartedness took my breath away. So I threw myself enthusiastically into the crowd. Then came the sound of the bell for church and the crowd of boys moved in a general rush. Not knowing what to do, I joined in the stampede, thinking that that was what you had to do. While I was scampering off, I fell into the arms of a young priest who was trying to stop the wave of youngsters running. It was Don Bosco. Smiling, he asked me, *What's your name?'* *Batistin* I said.

That memory of that meeting lasted thirty-eight years, until Don Bosco's death. Batistin Francesia would become a well-known Salesian. He wrote *A Short and Popular Life of Don Bosco*[46] which made the saintly priest of Turin known to hundreds of thousands of people.

To Batistin we owe the most familiar and intimate memories of the life of Don Bosco and his mother, he lived with them for seven years. Don Bosco discovered his intellectual ability, and with his mother's permission took him out of the foundry and persuaded him to study. He became the first teacher in the Oratory to obtain a degree, a Latinist of renown, the author of hundreds of books and pamphlets that made Don Bosco and his work known all round the world.

We had complete confidence in her, as if we were her children

Fr Batistin Francesia later wrote:

> His mother enjoyed a good reputation among anyone who knew her, as a mother who looked after her sons, bringing them up in a Christian way. Having known her for seven years at the Oratory, I found that this reputation was not exaggerated. She dressed modestly as a simple country woman, looked after the day-to-day organisation of the Oratory, was a mother to all and was called *Mamma* by everyone. When Don Bosco introduced some stranger to her, she seemed so shy and humble. It is my opinion that this good woman was a little overwhelmed in her later years, feeling she couldn't cope with all

---

[46] Vita Breve e Popolare di Don Bosco

the work with the increase in numbers of boys. When I became one of the boarders, in 1852, there were between thirty and forty of us. She often went to Don Bosco to say, *There is so much to be done and I just can't do any more!* To which he would reply, *Take it easy and don't work too hard! What you cannot do we will get others to do.* In her old age Don Bosco gave her all the attention she deserved. We boys called her Mamma Margaret, and we had every confidence in her, as if we were her children. We were especially impressed by her virtues and her exemplary life.

His mother's proverbs

During a rainy autumn and long winter, Mamma Margaret's kitchen was a refuge, with welcoming warmth and affection. She was always there, peeling potatoes, washing the rice, darning socks, saying the rosary, while the pots were slowly bubbling away. The boys used to go and sit near her, looking for some extra bread and affection. We owe it again to Batistin for what we know of that warm little corner of her world:

One day a small boy came and sat on a stool near her, and started to cry, telling her how his friends were teasing him. She offered him a bunch of grapes and said: *It's a hard life, isn't it?* And after some moments they started laughing together.

Mamma Margaret was reprimanding one of the bigger boys who was kicking a book around like a football. After a while she realised he was embarrassed, and murmured: *After an injury you need to pour on oil!* And she gave him an apple.

A hungry boy was helping himself to a piece of cheese while he was talking to her. Mamma Margaret was cleaning the lettuces, but she was watching him out of the corner of her eye, and she said to him severely: *Nice one! Conscience is like a small itch. Some feel it, some don't.*

One boy, asked by Don Bosco many times to make his confession, confided in her, *If I could find the right priest who would be sympathetic, I would. But I've never found one!* She reminded him of the old Piedmontese proverb, *A fussy washerwoman can never find the right stone to do the washing on.*[47]

One young boy had become aggressive, always upset, was a nuisance to the others. Margaret, seeing him go by, called him from the window. She made him sit near her, gave him an apple then said to him quietly, *Now I have to tell*

---

[47] Na cativa lavandera, trova mai na buna pera

you something very important. Your mother would probably tell you the same thing. Do you know you have changed? Why are you becoming so difficult? If you would like to know why, I can tell you: You are no longer praying. You are always the last one to go to church. Poor you, if God cannot help you, what good can you do in life? Eat your apple and think about it. There are so many other boys who behave well, happy to pray in church and do their homework. And Mamma looked at him with her quiet smile, her look all kindness and compassion.

Bravo, she said to one boy, *I'm so proud of you.* And to another, *Don Bosco is happy with you, the Lord is happy too.* And to a third, tired of studying for a long time, she whispered, *Think of your reward in heaven, bravo!*

When the warmer weather came, Mamma Margaret would get out of the kitchen as soon as she could. She would sit out the front, the basket of washing to be mended next to her, the pot of rice to wash, the potatoes to clean. The boys playing would run past her and smile. One of them, tired, would stop for a while and give her a hand, cleaning the potatoes. The chickens rummaging in the grass would also come near, looking for a worm, or some grain. Someone would run past and for a joke would scare the chickens. The chickens would jump and fly off. Margaret, laughing, would say to the boy, *If you do that they won't lay any more eggs.*

This is Eugenio Reffo's impression of her in 1852. He was a boy who had come to the Oratory just to meet a friend, and along with Murialdo would become the Co-founder of the Giuseppini.[48]

I can still visualise today Don Bosco's mother, Margaret, standing at the entrance to the kitchen there on the ground floor, near the Chapel, washing the rice for those first pupils. I can still see her in her country dress with her headscarf, looking so friendly.[49] Reason, religion, loving-kindness are the three values which sum up Don Bosco's preventive system. He learned them and continued to learn them from his mother. The great Salesian Work that would grow so vigorously from this cottage and courtyard, began on Mamma Margaret's knees.

---

[48] Society of Saint Joseph of Turin

[49] E Reffo, Quello che ricordo

Grigio

Batistin Francesia, at the time when Turin was hunting down priests, sometimes saw the mysterious dog Don Bosco called *Grigio*, and which often saved his life. He writes:

> I can still see the dog, scratching on the door to be let in, then coming into the little room where Don Bosco was eating. He would offer him something to eat but he would never take it. He would do a lap around the table, stretch out for a while at Don Bosco's feet, then go off. On one occasion the doorkeeper was frightened by it and hit him on the back. The animal took the blow, yelped, then ran off. Don Bosco called him *Grigio* because of the colour of his fur, and that's the name he was known by in the Oratory, that dear saviour of our Don Bosco.

Mamma Margaret always looked on the big dog with a degree of alarm. When she saw it she would cry, *Oh, that ugly beast!* But on one occasion she was very grateful it was around. John Bonetti tells the story:

> Because he had forgotten something during the day, Don Bosco had to go out one evening rather late. Mamma Margaret tried to talk him out of it, because thieves had already tried to attack him of an evening. He told her not to worry, and asked some boys to go with him into the city. He began to walk down the steps. Grigio was stretched out on the bottom step. He tried to move him out of the way, then jumped over him. But the big dog kept growling and pulling him back. Mamma Margaret, at the top of the steps, saw it all and said, *If you won't listen to me, then listen to the dog at least: Don't go out!* Don Bosco obeyed. The following day he found out that there was a hired assassin in the district waiting for him.

Who was that dog that disappeared at a certain point? One day Baronness Azeglia Ricci-Fassati asked Don Bosco that question, and he shrugged his shoulders, *I've no idea. It would be laughable to suggest that he was my guardian angel with a face like that! But I don't think he was just an ordinary dog.*

32. Cholera Epidemic

Buzzetti

Little by little, as Mamma Margaret grew older and the boarding section increased in numbers, Don Bosco made sure that she got some help. The first was Joseph Buzzetti, a boy with a shy smile, who had come into the city with his two brothers from Caronno Varesino. He was too weak to be a bricklayer like them, and Don Bosco took him away from bricks and mortar and brought him to Valdocco. He was fourteen. He said to him, *Help my mother in whatever way you can.* So Joseph became a little Oratory manager. Don Bosco trusted him like he would himself, and Mamma Margaret loved him like her own son. She saw him grow up next to her and do all the difficult jobs for ten years, until the end of her days. *Much of the story of the first Oratory,* John Bonetti wrote, *I got from Joseph Buzzetti who lived with Don Bosco from those earliest days. Her sister Marianna was a great help in the laundry. Chatting and laughing between loads they would relive the lively days of their childhood.*

Margaret Gastaldi, mother of the future Archbishop of Turin, often came to give a hand, together with her sister and daughter. They looked after the boys' linen and cleaning. She used be known as *the Mother General*, because of her authority and briskness, as she would stop a boy, straighten up his clothes, examine his collar, inspect his ears, then, *Go and wash! Immediately.* Some other very good women would come down to the Oratory to help, including Marchesa Fassati and Don Rua's mother, Giovanna Maria.

On August 14th 1854, the first priest who would help and stay with Don Bosco forever, came down from Avigliana. His name was Vittorio Alasonatti, for many years a primary school teacher, and when his friend Don Bosco insisted with much loving-kindness, he stopped teaching there and came to the Oratory. Don Bosco embraced him gratefully, and took to him to Mamma Margaret, *You will no longer have to worry about accounts, debts and expenditure. This good priest Don Vittorio Alasonatti will take care of all that.*

There was certainly a need for it. The young boarders were now nearly fifty in number. Joseph Buzzetti needed to spend a good amount of time in the city doing the shopping. Mamma Margaret, feeling her 66 years of age, could not do much more.

Cholera has broken out!

The day after his arrival, Don Alasonatti had just set up his little bursar's office when he received a strange urgent call: to give the Last Sacraments to some poor man, dying of cholera. This fatal epidemic had already struck the city of Genoa, leaving three thousand dead. In Turin, on July 30th, the first cases were diagnosed in Borgo Dora, where there were open drains.

While the King and the Royal Family could escape to their castle at Caselette, (some example of royal courage!) Mayor Notta found himself dealing with a city where the number who had caught the disease reached 800 in a month. Without any infrastructure for dealing with an epidemic of this kind, except for some old quarantine stations, the mayor made an appeal to the good-will of volunteers. Don Bosco mobilised his older boys, those over fourteen, guaranteeing their immunity if they remained in the friendship of the Lord. Mamma Margaret prepared a bottle of vinegar for each of them, giving it to them, saying, *After you have attended a sick person, wash your hands with the vinegar. When the bottle is empty, come and have it refilled. Now be sure: Follow my directions, because the Lord says, God helps those who help themselves.*

These were hot and heavy days. Cholera is a filthy and unpleasant disease, causing vomiting and diarrhoea. As a result the young helpers often found the sick without clean sheets and linen. When they returned to refill their bottles of vinegar they told Mamma Margaret. She gave them the few things they had at the Oratory but very soon there was nothing left. One day a boy came back and said frantically, *We have to take a seriously sick person to the Quarantine, but we haven't got any decent sheets. Have you got something, Mamma?* Margaret thought about it, then went and got the altar cloth from the altar and gave it to him, *Take this for your sick person. I don't think the Lord will mind.*

The story of Pietro Enria

Pietro Enria was a boy, thirteen years of age. In Borgo Dora, in the decrepit old house his family rented, he saw his mother die of cholera and his father become seriously ill. He and his four brothers were left with nobody and nothing. Two of the men from the *Cholera Committee* found them, and brought them to the *orphan refuge* at the Church of Saint Dominic. Families intending to adopt someone would go there. In September Don Bosco went there too. Pietro described:

> I had never seen him before. He was smiling and full of kindness. This made you love him even before he began to speak to you. He smiled at all of us. Eventually he came near me, and I felt my heart pumping. He asked me my name and surname, then said to me, *Do you want to come with me? We will*

always be friends until we go to heaven.[50] And I answered *Oh yes, Sir.* Then he added, *Is this your brother with you?* I answered. *Yes, Sir.* With a smile he said, *Well, he can come too.*

A few days later the two of us were brought to the Oratory. I was then thirteen and my brother eleven. From that point on I always remained at the Oratory, where he and his mother lovingly welcomed us, and we looked on Don Bosco's mother as ours too, and had great love for her. She was a woman of great piety and burning charity, more than just a mother. If someone was home from work, she would help him with a mother's love. When Don Bosco needed to be away preaching outside Turin, she did everything. We were content and happy at the Oratory.

Pietro Enria had occasion to speak to Don Bosco about those days, while he was helping him during his serious illness seventeen years later in Varazze:

Do you remember, Don Bosco, when your mother used tell you off when you took in new boys? She used say, *You take in new boys; but how are you going to look after and clothe them? There is nothing here and it is getting cold.* And in fact in my case, I had just arrived, and I had to sleep for some nights on a pile of leaves with nothing but a small blanket over me. In the evenings when we went to bed, you and your mother would mend our torn clothes, because that was all we had. Don Bosco smiled hearing that and said, *How hard my good mother worked! She was a holy woman! But providence never failed us.*

I'll Take Them All

In the first days of December 1854 the City authorities declared the cholera over and deaths from it at an end. In the Saint Dominic's refuge a lot of families had come to adopt one of the orphans and as usually happens had picked the *best of the bunch.* About twenty children were left over, the smallest, the unwanted. Don Bosco went and brought them all to the Oratory. They followed him around holding him by the hand, chirping like little chicks. Don Bosco set up a separate class for them, gave them a good teacher. In a request he made, on November 13th to the Barolo Institute, he wrote:

I find myself in difficult circumstances. I have to look after some of the poorest and most abandoned, because of the many boys left orphaned and abandoned during the sad cholera epidemic. Because I am in need, I am turning to you respectfully and in trust, begging you to note the state of complete abandon these poor young boys find themselves in, and I am asking for your help.

---

[50] In Piedmontese, *Saruma amis – fin ch'anduma 'n Paradis*

The situation really was an exceptional one. The mayor also wrote to Don Bosco thanking him and promising him help from the city funds. Since they were all little children, the other boarders laughingly called them *the lower class*. They sought out Mamma Margaret as their mother, surrounded her, loved her deeply. Amongst them, with her tender smile she was like Snow White and a multitude of dwarfs. She embraced them, wiped their noses and felt that she was once more, as she was at The Becchi, a poor but happy grandmother.

A Mother's Prayer

Winter 1854-55 was a cold winter. Pietro Enria recalls, *In the mornings, at Mass, the church was so cold that at times Don Bosco had frozen hands and he could hardly hold the chalice.* Mamma Margaret was there every day in the first bench, asking the Lord for the strength and the means to persevere, with an ever more numerous family.

She not only prayed in church. Thinking of God throughout the day was part of her thanksgiving after Mass. She had never read nor heard the Fathers of the Church, but in her life, she practised the kind of prayer, which Saint John Chrysostom had explained to his Christians 1500 years before:

Prayer should not be determined by set moments or hours, but flourish continuously day and night. There is no need, in fact, to raise our minds to God only when we concentrate on prayer with all our spirit. We need to have the desire for and remind ourselves of God, also when we are busy with other things, be it in looking after the poor or other activities so that, seasoned by God's love, like salt, everything becomes food for the Lord of the Universe.

33. The Final Years

In 1853 Don Bosco succeeded in completing the construction of a new building, next to the house bought from Pinardi. His intention was to open workshops in the Oratory for boys who were going to work for employers in town. The main reason was, *To protect the boys, from bad habits and bad company*, which were part of daily work situations. Pietro Enria, for whom Don Bosco had found work with an ironmonger, recalls:

> How many times I had to get out of the workshop to avoid obscene conversations from older boys who were men really. I was only fourteen. Two of them were particularly bad. They felt no shame in speaking badly of religion. They were like two animals as far as their habits were concerned.

Don Bosco began slowly, as always. And as always, with Mamma Margaret's help. In the autumn of 1853 he opened the first workshops: for shoemakers and tailors. The first one was sited close to church of St Francis de Sales, and he himself looked after that. The second one was near the kitchen, and Mamma Margaret took responsibility for that. She only taught the simple things, which all housewives at the time knew. But Don Bosco gave her a hand, remembering that John Roberto of Castelnuovo, the tailor, had once encouraged him *to put his books away*, and be a proper tailor.

In the first months of 1854 he opened the third workshop, bookbinding. Bookbinding began rather primitively. A small group of boys, under Don Bosco's guidance, had folded a large set of sixteen pages. Then they folded others and placed them one on top of the other. *The book is finished!* Don Bosco announced triumphantly. *Now we only need to stitch it and glue on the cover.* Mamma Margaret, called to help, brought a needle and strong thread, and a tin of glue made from flour. With the needle they managed to sew the folded pages together. The glue bound the cover around them, but the edges had to be trimmed. After a few unsuccessful attempts, Mamma Margaret said, *Leave it to me*. She went to the kitchen and came back with the sharp knife she used to slice the carrots and onions. Three smart cuts, and the book was trimmed properly. Mamma Margaret, Don Bosco and the boys all laughed. In this way, the book-binding workshop was launched.

At The Becchi: How things had changed

In autumn 1854, once the cholera was over, Don Bosco went with his mother and some of the better boys to The Becchi, to celebrate the feast of Our Lady of the Rosary. Mamma Margaret embraced her loved ones. It seemed impossible that her grandchildren had grown so much, some of them taller than her. She saw the old cottage again, and the room where she slept with her children, and where John, as a small boy, had that dream from which his life had unravelled, like a skein of wool. It was Our Lady who enlightened his mind with that dream. She thought again of his description; the courtyard, the crowd of boys fighting and cursing, she had seen so many of them around the streets of Borgo Dora! Wild animals turned into lambs, she had seen that happen slowly but surely during their time in their new home, in the big church which had arrived miraculously on the scene.

For those few days she went to stay with Joseph, and prayed in the little chapel Joseph had built on the left-hand corner of the ground floor, a few paces from the stretch of land where John tied a rope between two trees for his first show, to get his first young friends to pray. How things had changed, and how she too had changed, now at sixty-six, gasping for breath as she climbed the path was something she never thought about as a young mother.

So much had improved. So many paddocks now sowed with corn and potatoes, food was never lacking at home. The houses themselves were larger, better. Even workers' wages in Turin had increased. They had noticed in recent months: a worker on twelve hours a day now earned two or two and a half lire a day. The women in the factories were now earning one lira, and boys, seventy cents. There was only one reason for this: five years without war, and things always went better when there was no war.

Dominic Savio

On October 2nd, a Monday, Don Bosco met Dominic Savio and his father at The Becchi. They came to ask if Dominic could be accepted at the Oratory. Don Bosco noticed the boy's poor health immediately, but was very taken by his intelligence, and especially by his love for the Lord. Don Bosco accepted him. They would see him in Turin. Dominic, came with his father, to the Oratory on October 29th.

There were many exceptional boys at the Oratory, boys like Michael Rua, John Cagliero, Camillo Gavio, Francis Cerruti. Don Bosco recognised that he was living *among young saints*. Mamma Margaret was aware of the same thing. When she paused from work to gain her breath, she would spend a few moments in the new church of St Francis de Sales, sitting in the last bench as one enters from the left. She would take out her Rosary and pray. As a young mother, her thoughts were for God, but also for her children. She would hear their voices and guess what they were saying, what they were doing, thinking. One day she said to Don Bosco. *You have so many good young people, but nobody surpasses the beauty of heart and mind of Dominic Savio.* Don Bosco asked her why, and she replied, *I've seen him pray. He stays behind in the chapel after the services are over. He often interrupts his games to come and find Jesus in the tabernacle. In church he stands there like an angel. Keep an eye on him, this is a very special young man.*[51]

They Called Her *Mamma*

In those final years, as well as Dominic, some other very good boys came to Valdocco. They spent a long time there and had their own memories of Mamma Margaret. John Baptist Anfossi had lost his father and his mother. He came to the Oratory on December 22nd 1853. He remained there until 1864. He became a priest and canon in Turin. He recalls:

> When I came, there were around fifty-one of us. I knew Don Bosco's mother for three years; we called her *Mamma*. I admired her life of sacrifice. She spent all her time on us children, and we felt she was our mother. When we needed something, we went to her, and she would bend over backwards to give us what we needed, exhorting us to pray and to be virtuous. Everyone who came to the Oratory held her in veneration, even people of high status. They admired her as a pious, charitable person always ready to help.

John Turchi was a boy from Castelnuovo whom Don Bosco brought to the Oratory in 1851. He stayed there ten years. He became a priest and a teacher at the seminary:

> I had heard from many people in the town that Margaret, Don Bosco's mother, was a truly Christian mother, solely concerned with her religious duties and wisely educating her family. I happened to live many years with her at the Oratory, and I saw how involved she was in helping her son with his works of charity, and how good and charitable she was with the youngsters at the Oratory.

John Villa, from Ponderano, Biella, came to Turin at a very young age in search of work. From 1855 he frequented the Festive Oratory for eleven years, and often went to confession there. He became a good father of his family and also helped Don Bosco financially:

> I knew Don Bosco's mother. She was an example of a good housewife, with a truly Christian spirit. At the Oratory she fulfilled the role of a good and pious mother for all of us. We all had the confidence of children in her: and we were especially edified by her virtues and her exemplary conduct. She told me, amongst other things, how Don Bosco taught his youngsters every kind of trade, starting from scratch, *He would cook and show them how to cook. He*

---

[51] Dominic Savio was canonised in1954

took my old aprons that I had hung up, to cut them up and make shorts for the boarders who needed them.

John Baptist Piano, from Caramagna, came to Valdocco in 1854. He was a companion of Dominic Savio. Later he became parish priest of the church of Gran Madre di Dio in Turin:

I knew Don Bosco's mother. Margaret was her name. She looked after the house finances in the Oratory and the kitchen, and we called her *Mamma*. Don Bosco, without a doubt, was blessed with exceptional help from his mother in setting up the Oratory. The devotion, the piety and the faith of Don Bosco's mother was the reason for Don Bosco's own virtue. One deserved the other.

34. From Kitchen to Heaven

During the autumn of 1856 Mamma Margaret became very tired. She almost never left the kitchen now, where she sat near the fire to work and pray. If you wanted to find her, that's where she would be. The children from the *lower class* played around her feet, looking for a smile and an apple. They were always famished. Many of them liked sitting with her, listening to her stories and watching her work. They felt the warmth of the home and a mother's warmth.

A Mother's Opinion

In 1835, so long ago, when he was twenty, the cleric John Bosco had climbed into the pulpit in Alfiano to give his first sermon. The parish priest, Don Joseph Pelato, when asked what he thought of it, congratulated the young cleric first of all, but then said that the people would not have understood the sermon. Standing there, he gave Don Bosco a formula for preaching that he would employ throughout his life, *Speak in a simple, very simple, popular way!* Now, at Valdocco, Don Bosco was not only preaching, but writing many books and pamphlets for the people. He wanted these to always be, *Simple, very simple, and popular.* For this reason he would go down to the kitchen every now and again with a handful of pages and say, *Mamma, keep working, and I will read these pages to you. You tell me when you understand and when you don't understand.*

One afternoon he came down with a handful of pages about the life of Saint Peter, the first Pope to whom Jesus had said, *I will give you the keys of the Kingdom of Heaven.* Don Bosco had chosen as a title, *The Great Clavigero* (The great Key bearer). As soon as she heard the title, Mamma Margaret said, Clavigero, where is that village? Don Bosco saw he had made a mistake, and changed the title to read, simply, *Saint Peter.*

Mamma Margaret is Unwell

In October 1856 Don Bosco went as usual to The Becchi for the celebration of Our Lady of the Rosary. He took some of the better boys with him. But for the first time Mamma Margaret did not go. She felt unwell. For some days she stayed in bed tormented by a persistent cough.

In the very early hours of the morning when first light filtered through the window, with a skein of wool and her knitting needles she began to knit a pair of socks for a boy who had none. But after a while she stopped. Her eyes were closing, and the cough was more persistent. Don Bosco called Doctor Bellingeri, and the diagnosis was not good, *Pneumonia*. This was the illness that had carried off Francis, her husband and years after, nearly carried off her son. For the elderly, at that time, *Pneumonia* meant *the end*. Mamma Margaret knew it, and she asked Don Bosco to call her confessor, Don Borel, and to bring her Viaticum.

Don Bosco immediately went to tell his brother Joseph, and gathered the boys together to pray for their very sick Mamma. Nobody expected this news. Everyone was in deep sorrow. Mothers never die. They were indestructible. To believe that a mother was no longer there was to believe that the sun shone no more, that the fields had no more grass. Impossible! How could anyone manage without her? In the small corridor near her room they clustered, especially the *lower class,* who wanted to see her, to listen to her. It was hard for Don Bosco to calmly tell them that it was not possible, that Mamma needed rest.

Your Turn to Help Your Mother

Don Bosco thought what a grave loss this would be for the Oratory, and especially for him. She had taught him how to live, how to be a priest, how to educate boys, and all this while they went off to the fields, when they would quietly talk in the evenings while she was stirring the polenta at the Oratory. She had taught him the wisdom of never giving up, of trusting in providence. She had given him, without his realising it, his educational system which the world marvelled at. This was all summed up in her life in the words, *Kindness, goodness, strength of a mother.*

Don Borel came to hear her confession, and then went to bring the Eucharist as Viaticum. She turned to her son, *When you were little, I helped you to receive Jesus. Now it is your turn to help your mother. Say the prayers out loud. I will repeat them after you.* Joseph came from The Becchi, his hands still soiled from work. She whispered to them like any mother, *Love one another.*

The next day, as the illness progressed, she managed to say to Don Bosco:
> *God knows how much I have loved you throughout my life. I hope to be able to love you even better in eternity. My conscience is clear. I have done my duty in everything I could. Look after your boys. Many, instead of God's glory, seek their own. Many love poverty in others, but not for themselves.* After a long pause, *Remember that in this life there is suffering. True pleasure is in eternal life.*

In these simple words Margaret had expressed the ideal of Christian life of hundreds of generations from the villages, the conviction that had helped thousands of mothers to keep going in life, despite famine and wars, the death of their children and crushing fatigue.

God came to take her to himself at 3 o'clock on the morning of November 25th. Don Bosco and Joseph threw themselves into each other's arms.

You Have to be Their Mother

Don Bosco, two hours later, asked Joseph Buzzetti to go with him to the Shrine of Our Lady, the Consolata. Joseph was his friend in these bitter moments, the only one Don Bosco was not ashamed to be seen crying with. He went to celebrate Mass in the crypt at the Shrine, and he prayed to Our Lady, *They have no mother. You have to be their mother.*

The simple parish records of the church of Saints Simon and Jude,[52] document the event:

> In the year of Our Lord 1856, on the 25th day of the month of November, at three in the morning in this parish, at the Bosco home, strengthened by the Sacraments, Margaret Bosco died, 69 years of age, native of Capriglio district. recorded by Don Joseph Alasonatti, 45 years of age, and Joseph Buzzetti, 24 years of age. The body was interred on November 26th in the Turin cemetery.

When the *primitivo a mezzanotte* cemetery plot,[53] where Mamma Margaret had been buried, was closed, her mortal remains were transferred to a general ossuary, like the rest of the poor of Turin.

---

[52] Now the church of Saint Joachim

[53] Row 31B grave no 117

35. Beyond the Horizon

Beyond the horizons of this poor mortal existence, there is another life, which Mamma Margaret called *eternal life,* which Jesus proclaimed with the words: Blessed are the poor, for theirs is the Kingdom of Heaven.[54]

Don Bosco relates how some years later he *saw* his mother. Don Lemoyne tells the story:
> In August 1860, Don Bosco appeared to meet up with his mother near the Shrine of the Consolata. She seemed to look so beautiful.
> *But how come! Is it you?* Don Bosco asked her.
> *I am dead but I am alive,* Mamma Margaret answered.
> *And are you happy?*
> *Extremely happy.*
> *Give me a sign of your happiness.*
> Then he saw his mother resplendent, dressed in precious clothes, with a look of wondrous majesty. Margaret began to sing. Her song spoke of love of God, of inexpressible sweetness, it went straight to the heart, enveloped him.

> Don Bosco, hearing that sweetest of all melodies, remained there enchanted. He no longer knew what to say or to ask his mother. Mamma Margaret, the song finished, turned to him and said:
> *I am waiting for you, since we two must always be together.*
> Having spoken these words, she disappeared.[55]

---

[54] Luke 6:20

[55] BM 5,375-6

36. Sequel

The Mother And The Cardinal

Some years ago I was accompanying Cardinal Joseph Ratzinger and Archbishop Tarcisio Bertone on a visit to places where Don Bosco had been, around Valdocco.

We had paused for a moment in the area where Mamma Margaret's garden had been. I told the story that this is where Mamma Margaret grew the vegetables that were the only dish available for Don Bosco and his boys. During one Sunday afternoon in 1850, at the height of the war games, the boys, who made up the *defeated army,* invaded the garden, and destroyed Mamma Margaret's precious plot, despite her vigorous protests as she watched the devastation from the small balcony.

All Salesians know that Mamma Margaret was very discouraged by this, and that she felt all of her 62 years weighing on her that afternoon. During the evening, together with Don Bosco, she was mending the shirts and shoes which the boys needed for the following morning. At a certain point she laid down her needle beside the oil lamp and said quietly: *John, I'm tired. Let me return to The Becchi. Every day they pull the clean washing off the line. Today they trod all over the garden, and I have no idea now what to put in the cooking pot. I'm a poor old woman. I just can't carry on any further. Let me go and spend the rest of my days with my grandchildren.* Don Bosco looked at his mother and felt a lump in his throat. He couldn't find a word to say. He just lifted his hand and pointed to the Crucifix hanging on the wall. His elderly mother understood. She bent her head once again to the task and kept sewing.

I ended on a quiet note and turned to the Cardinal: *If there is holiness in ecstasy and visions, there's also holiness in washing pots and mending shoes.* We walked on no more than ten metres, and reached the staircase that would bring us up to Don Bosco's rooms. The Cardinal was in deep thought. After climbing a few steps he stopped, and said to me animatedly: *But why haven't you made this mother a Saint?* Half in jest, I replied, *Your Eminence, you know that in the Vatican, until not so long ago, not much thought was given to mothers of families.* He waved his right arm as if he was brushing flies away: *But now many things have changed,* he said.

Many things have changed, even in the Vatican. Amongst other things, Cardinal Joseph Ratzinger has become Pope Benedict XVI. It is my hope that Mamma Margaret's place, maybe by the will of this Pope, will change, from being a humble *Mamma* hidden in the shadow of her great son, to *Blessed* offered to the people of God as a model for mothers and those who serve poor and abandoned young people.

In this book I have attempted to trace the delicate threads of the heroism of Mamma Margaret, for she was a great woman, but only in the eyes of God and the poor. In just a few pages it is not possible to describe fully the life of a great woman. It is easy to describe the life of a general or a scientist, but not so easy for an outstanding mother. The holiness of a mother lies in the heroism of the bits and pieces that make up the 365 days of the year. It is not made up of outstanding events. Mamma Margaret's heroism lay in feeding poor boys with soup and affection, of mending worn-out clothes, of washing pots and pans. In those humble moments lay the strength of a life lived as a Christian, all based on the cheerfulness of the poor, on innate common sense, on a real trust in Divine Providence.

Teresio Bosco
August 27th 2005
Feast of St Monica

MAMMA MARGARET'S LIFE CHRONICLE

1788	April 1st.	Margaret Occhiena born Capriglio, Asti
1811	February 28th.	Wife of Francis Bosco dies.
1812	June 6th.	Margaret Occhiena marries Francis Bosco.
1813	April 8th.	Birth of first child, Joseph.
1815	August 16th.	Birth of second child, John.
1817	February 8th.	Francis acquires the stable at the Becchi.
1817	May 11th.	Francis Bosco dies of pneumonia.
1817	November	Margaret leaves the Biglione tenant quarters.
1818	March	Death of Margaret's mother, Domenica.
1820-1830		Margaret prepares her three sons for their First Confession and First Holy Communion.
1824		John has the dream that will change his life.
1824-1826		Margaret sends John to primary school
1826	February 11th.	Death of Margaret Zucca, Margaret's mother-in-law.
1826	Easter	John makes his First Communion.
1826 or 1827	February	John goes to the Moglia farm.
1829	November	John returns home and meets Don Calosso.
1830	November 21st.	Don Calosso dies suddenly. John starts school again in Castelnuovo.
1831	March 22nd.	Anthony marries Anna Rosso.
1831	November	John begins his secondary schooling in Chieri.
1833	March 9th.	Joseph marries Maria Calosso.
1835	October 30th.	John enters the Chieri seminary.
1839	October	Margaret returns to The Becchi.
1841	June 5th.	John is ordained priest in Turin.
1841-1846		Don Bosco founds his Oratory.
1846	July	Don Bosco falls seriously ill with pneumonia.
1846	October	Don Bosco asks his mother to come with him *to be a mother to his boys.*
1846	November 3rd.	Mother and son arrive in Valdocco.
1847	May	Mamma Margaret takes in the first boy.
1850		Mamma Margaret's garden is destroyed.
1849	January 18th.	Anthony dies at just 41 years of age.
1851-52		Don Bosco builds the church of St. Francis de Sales.
1852	April 26th.	The Turin Powder Works explodes.
1853		Don Bosco with the help of Mamma Margaret begins his own workshops.
1854	July	Cholera breaks out in Turin.
1854	Autumn	Don Bosco entrusts to Mamma Margaret twenty small boys orphaned by the cholera.
1854	October 29th.	Dominic Savio arrives at the Oratory.
1856	October	Mamma Margaret feels unwell.
1856	November 24th.	The doctor diagnoses pneumonia.
1856	November 25th.	3 am Mamma Margaret dies.

BIBLIOGRAPHY

Texts employed in writing this book

CONGREGATIO DE CAUSIS SANCTORUM P N 2029. Margaritae Occhiena vid. Bosco.

Positio, Vol. I e II, Roma 2000.

G BATTISTA LEMOYNE, Mamma Margaret, la Madre di S Giovanni Bosco, SEI 1956.

BREVE CATECHISMO Torino, reprinted 1888.

GIOVANNI BONETTI, Cinque lustri della storia dell'Oratorio Salesiano. Torino 1892

DOMENICO RUFFINO, Cronaca 1860 -1865.

SECONDO CASELLE, I Bosco di Chieri… LAS, Roma 1975.

FRANÇOIS DESRAMAUT Les Memorie I de Giovanni Battista Lemoyne, Lyon 1961.

Lemoyne, Amadei, Ceria Memorie biografiche di Don Giovanni Bosco, Bosco, 18 volumes Torino.

SAC GIOVANNI BOSCO, Memorie dell'Oratorio di S.Francesco di Sales dal 1815 al 1855, a cura di Eugenio Ceria, reprinted by Editrice SDB.

English - Memoirs of the Oratory (Don Bosco Publications New Rochelle 1989)

SAN GIOVANNI BOSCO, Memorie, trascrizione di T Bosco, Elledici, Leumann 1985.

GIOVANNI BOSCO, Scritti pedagogici e spirituali, LAS Roma1987.

MICHELE MOLINERIS, Don Bosco inedito, con albero genealogico dei Bosco, Colle Don Bosco, 1972.

PIETRO STELLA, Don Bosco nella storia della religiosità cattolica, I – III. LAS Rome, 1979.1981. 1988.

PIETRO STELLA, Don Bosco nella storia economica e sociale (1815-1870), LAS Roma 1980

G B FRANCESIA, Vita breve e popolare del venerabile Giovanni Bosco, Scuola Tipografica Salesiana, Torino 1907.

F GIRAUDI, L'Oratorio di Don Bosco, Torino 1933.

DICASTERO PER LA FORMAZIONE, Sussidi 1,2,3, Pro-manuscripto

JOAN SANTAEULARIA I GUITART, Cronologia completa de las Memorias Biograficas de San Juan Bosco, obra inedita. Barcelona 1979.

A GIRAUDO - G BIANCARDI, Qui è vissuto Don Bosco, Elledici, Leumann 1988. 2004.

GIACOMO DACQUINO, Psicologia di don Bosco, SEI Torino 1988.

NATALE CERRATO, Vi presento Don Bosco, Elledici, Leumann 2005

UMBERTO LEVRA, L'altro volto di Torino risorgimentale 1814-1848, Istituto per la Storia del Risorgimento Italiano, Torino 1988.

CLAUDIO FELLONI e ROBERTO AUDISIO, I giovani discoli, Archivio Storico della Città di Torino, Torino 1988.

MICHELE RUGGIERO, La storia dei briganti piemontesi (1796-1814), Piemonte in bancarella. Turin 1983